OSCAR WILDE

# THE PICTURE
# OF DORIAN GRAY

ADAPTED BY NEIL BARTLETT

D1334076

The Abbey Theatre gratefully acknowledges the financial
support of the Arts Council / An Chomhairle Ealaíon.

# ABBEY THEATRE
## Amharclann na Mainistreach

**The Abbey Theatre is Ireland's national theatre.** It was founded by W.B. Yeats and Lady Augusta Gregory. Since it first opened its doors in 1904 the theatre has played a vital and often controversial role in the literary, social and cultural life of Ireland.

The Abbey produces an annual programme of diverse, engaging, innovative Irish and international theatre and invests in and promotes new Irish writers and artists.

We do this by placing the writer and theatre-maker at the heart of all that we do, commissioning and producing exciting new work and creating discourse and debate on the political, cultural and social issues of the day. Our aim is to present great theatre in a national context so that the stories told on stage have a resonance with artists and audiences alike.

Over the years, the Abbey Theatre has nurtured and premiered the work of major playwrights such as J.M. Synge and Sean O'Casey as well as contemporary classics from the likes of Sebastian Barry, Marina Carr, Bernard Farrell, Brian Friel, Thomas Kilroy, Tom MacIntyre, Frank McGuinness, Tom Murphy, Mark O'Rowe, Billy Roche and Sam Shepard. We also support the new generation of Irish writers at the Abbey Theatre, including Carmel Winters, Nancy Harris, Elaine Murphy, Stacey Gregg and Gary Duggan.

None of this can happen without our audiences and our benefactors. Annie Horniman provided crucial financial support to the Abbey in its first years. And many others have followed her lead by investing in and supporting our work.

Thank you.

## ABBEY THEATRE BOARD OF DIRECTORS

Dr. Bryan McMahon (*Chairman*), Jane Brennan, Paul Davis, Moya Doherty, John Finnegan Róise Goan, Thomas Kilroy, James McNally, Mark Ryan

## ABBEY THEATRE SENIOR MANAGEMENT TEAM

Fiach Mac Conghail (*Director / CEO*), Declan Cantwell (*Director of Finance & Administration*) Oonagh Desire (*Director of Public Affairs & Development*), Gavin Harding (*Technical Director*) Aideen Howard (*Literary Director*)

Is í Amharclann na Mainistreach amharclann náisiúnta na hÉireann. W.B. Yeats agus an Bantiarna Augusta Gregory a bhunaigh í. Bhí, agus tá, ról ríthábhachtach agus go deimhin, ról a bhí sách conspóideach go minic, ag an amharclann i saol liteartha, sóisialta agus cultúrtha na hÉireann ó d'oscail sí a doirse den chéad uair i 1904.

Léiríonn Amharclann na Mainistreach clár amharclannaíochta as Éirinn agus ó thíortha thar lear in aghaidh na bliana atá ilghnéitheach, tarraingteach agus nuálach agus infheistíonn sí a cuid acmhainní i nua-scríbhneoirí agus nua-ealaíontóirí na hÉireann agus cuireann sí chun cinn iad.

Déanaimid é sin tríd an scríbhneoir agus an t-amharclannóir a chur i gcroílár an uile ní a dhéanaimid, trí shaothar nua spreagúil a choimisiúnú agus a léiriú agus trí dhioscúrsa agus díospóireacht a chruthú i dtaobh cheisteanna polaitiúla, cultúrtha agus sóisialta na linne. Is é atá mar aidhm again ealaín amharclannaíochta den scoth a láithriú i gcomhthéacs náisiúnta ionas go mbeidh dáimh ag lucht ealaíne agus lucht féachana araon leis na scéalta a bhíonn á n-aithris ar an stáitse.

In imeacht na mblianta, rinne Amharclann na Mainistreach saothar mórdhrámadóirí ar nós J.M. Synge agus Sean O'Casey a chothú agus a chéadléiriú, mar a rinne sí freisin i gcás clasaicí comhaimseartha ó dhrámadóirí amhail Sebastian Barry, Marina Carr, Bernard Farrell, Brian Friel, Thomas Kilroy, Tom MacIntyre, Frank McGuinness, Tom Murphy, Mark O'Rowe, Billy Roche agus Sam Shepard. Leanamid de thacnaíocht a thabhairt do scribhneoireacht nua in Amharclann na Mainistreach tríd ár bproíseas coimisiúnaithe agus ár gclár nua do dhrámadóirí.

Ní féidir aon ní den chineál sin a thabhairt i gcrích gan ár lucht féachana agus na deontóirí a thugann cabhair airgid dúinn. Sholáthair Annie Horniman tacaíocht airgid ríthábhachtach don Mhainistir siar i mblianta tosaigh na hamharclainne. Agus lean iliomad daoine eile an dea-shampla ceannródaíochta sin uaithi ó shin trí infheistíocht a dhéanamh inár gcuid oibre agus tacaíocht a thabhairt dúinn.

Go raibh maith agaibh.

# INTRODUCTION
Neil Bartlett

## 'Those who go beneath the surface do so at their peril'
Dorian Himself

When you tell people that you are going to put Wilde's *The Picture of Dorian Gray* on
the stage, they all promptly ask the same question; 'So what does he look like?'

By way of an answer, I would merely point out to anyone considering casting the role
that Dorian's much-vaunted looks are, in the book, never described beyond a few
generalities. They exist almost entirely in the variously smitten eyes of his beholders.
What matters is what he *does* with those looks. Convention dictates that what is
required for the part is a sort of glacial facial perfection and immobility – the approach
made iconic by Hurd Hatfield in the 1945 MGM movie – but in fact what you need is a
credibly twenty-year-old actor who can convincingly transform himself from a gauche
innocent into a drug-addicted middle-aged psychopath. The point about Dorian is not
that he doesn't change, but rather that he *does* change – and horribly. Paradoxically,
the gothic element of the plot that ought to be the hardest to bring off – the uncanny
miracle that as the years advance Dorian acquires not one wrinkle – is, in a theatre
performance, simply a given. Of course Dorian doesn't look any older on the day Lord
Henry Wotton dies than on the day that he met him, it's only been less than two hours
plus an interval since they first set eyes on each other.

Ideally, Dorian's looks, like his money and class, must be got out of the way in the very
first scene. They must be suggestive, not prescriptive. Only then can we concentrate
on the how, not the why, of his Faustian career. Above all, we must never see Dorian
making too much of an effort to seduce either the audience or the other characters. Like
those of his female counterpart, Wedekind's inexplicably attractive Lulu, his admirers
must come to him already clutching their own deaths.

## *'All art is at once surface and symbol'*
### The Picture

The second question that people ask – usually in gleeful anticipation of throwing you into a panicked tangle of bluff and promise – is; 'So, how are you going to do the picture?'

Well, every production must find its own solution, and much as I would hope that any future production of this script will pay little regard to my stage directions and concentrate on finding its own response to the imagery of the original story, this adaptation does come with a built-in proposition as to how the picture of the title is to be realised. (Please note; if you are an audience member reading this introduction before you see the show tonight, then it might be wise to stop reading now). One of the strongest tricks of Wilde's story is its suggestiveness – indeed, in some crucial ways the story might even be said to be *about* the power of suggestion. As Lord Henry Wotton puts it in the speech that triggers Dorian's fatal wish that he may never age, 'It is in the brain, and the brain only, that the great sins of the world take place....' And Lord Henry is right; almost all of the novel's horrors are left – cleverly and insidiously – to the reader's deliberately inflamed imagination. Every crime that Dorian is accused of – the drugs, the suicides, the homosexuality, the bisexuality, the orgies, the adultery, the blackmail – remain, largely, just that, accusations. Little is laid down in black and white, much is hinted at – in confessions, in salacious hints, in gossip and in rumour. With the exception of Basil Hallward's murder, we never actually see him at work on anyone's flesh. Likewise, the picture of the title is mostly left in the mind's eye. Basil's style of painting for instance is left completely unspecified – is he as radical an artist as Wilde's contemporary Whistler was, or as skilfully formulaic as Carolus Duran – or as somewhere-in-between as John Singer Sargeant, in whose work flattery and authenticity are often indistinguishable? We are never told. Although the very first changes to his masterpiece's painted surface are subtly and economically evoked, it is never thereafter described in anything approaching detail – even the family portraits that hang in Dorian's country house are more accurately described. This trick of suggestiveness works a very particular kind of spell, and one that is essential to the story's success. By making his readers imagine the corruption of the picture, Wilde makes us subtly and uncannily complicit in that corruption, and therefore in Dorian's also. The logic is that of all seducers: if we can imagine his sins, then surely we can also imagine committing them ourselves – and if we can imagine that, then surely on some (perhaps unconscious?) level that must mean that we *want* to commit them? That is why, in this staging, the picture is done *suggestively*; with nothing but Wilde's original words. Like a conjuror insisting that he has nothing up his sleeve, my script starts the evening by showing the audience a provocatively blank (if diabolically black) canvas. Then, every time that Dorian looks at it, the actors paint that canvas with strokes and fragments of Wilde's prose. Simple as that.

This device also has the great virtue of economy. It means that the budget can be spent on actors, not in the props department. It also honours the fact that it is to hear Wilde's language that people have bought their tickets, not to see a bit of scene painting or (these days) a video installation. It is his way with words that an audience wants to experience – that extraordinary, idiosyncratic phrasing, with its apparently undiminished ability (in both its high comic and the lower, melodramatic, gothic modes) to outrage propriety and embody transgression.

## *'It is the spectator, and not life, that art really mirrors'*
### The Chorus

All through his life, Wilde was obsessed with the idea of tragedy. In *De Profundis*, he tried to re-shape his messy, catastrophic affair with Douglas into a downfall of tragic proportions and trajectory, explicitly comparing himself at one point to a figure out of Sophocles. In *Salome*, he tried to seriously re-invent poetic tragedy as a valid contemporary theatrical form, and very nearly succeeded. Not content to be creatures of melodrama merely, the secret-riddled heroes and heroines of all of his plays (even of *The Importance*; who is Lady Bracknell, if not Nemesis herself?) often speak of themselves as being dogged by almost classical Furies of guilt and terror. This obsession was where I found my alibi for the idea that the passages of prose describing the picture should be spoken not by characters, but by the company stepping out of character and acting as a chorus. And once the company had become a chorus, I knew I then had a way of realising the extraordinarily suggestive (that word again) manner in which the novel both celebrates and damns its hero. Because it is always both within and without the action, a chorus's function must always necessarily be ambiguous. In this case, the more they claim to be taking a merely documentary, story-telling approach to the proceedings – the more they insist that they are only there to act as witnesses and supply the odd fact or suggestion – the more they betray the fact that they seem to be somehow relishing their allotted task of personally chivvying, luring and tricking

Dorian to his pre-ordained death. To put it bluntly, they seem to feel about Dorian the same way as we do. They seem to know – somehow – that we want the pleasure of seeing this beautiful young man dare to commit all of these sins on our behalf, but also at the same time want the pleasure of seeing him appallingly punished (on our behalf) for committing them. Or should that be the other way round?

When they speak in their function as chorus, this script suggests that on occasion the ensemble drop the accents – the masks, if you like – of their characters. When the piece is produced elsewhere, this will have its own fresh implications, but in the auditorium of the Abbey, Ireland's national theatre, the room for which this adaptation was created, this switch of accent had a very specific and entirely intentional effect. It meant hearing Wilde as an Irish voice. I knew from having already staged *An Ideal Husband* with a company of Irish actors at the Abbey that Irish voices of all kinds and classes often bring a peculiarly apt energy to Wilde's writing, despite (or perhaps because of) the fact that they have to deliver it in what is, to them, a foreign accent. As any voice coach will tell you, there are two elements to successfully assuming an accent which is not naturally your own; you have to get both the accent itself right, and (perhaps more importantly) you have to grasp this foreign voice's essential music. Although the *accent* of Wilde's writing is always that of his adopted London, the *music* (to my ear at least, and at least below the surface) is often deeply Irish. The trademark paradoxes aside, in his prose and in the longer speeches of his stage dialogue especially, there is often something in the sheer loquacity, in the sense of language as performance and especially in the highly distinctive drive through the full-stops to that all-important end of an extended paragraph that is a whole Irish Sea away from the clipped, tightly-corseted linguistic protocols of Belgravia and Chelsea. When it came to the "voicing" of the picture in this script, I simply wanted to unleash some of that music. I am well aware that this apparently simple shift of voice is in fact far from simple, and that it sets up all sorts of other echoes, and begs all sort of other questions. But in this story which is so much about surface and what lies beneath it, so much about what can and can't be left behind when one re-invents oneself, it seemed entirely legitimate to make the public voices of Dorian's world as scrupulously and artificially English as possible, while letting his most private life resonate with some of the sounds which his creator so ruthlessly ironed out of his own public voice when he emigrated and re-invented himself as the voice of not just society, but Society.

## '*To reveal art and conceal the artist is art's aim*'
### Dorian as Autobiography

Because he has been for over a century an artist whose life is as famous – if not more famous – than his work, *Dorian* is a story which audiences are keen to read autobiographically. This is not a modern phenomenon. As early as 1890, when the book first appeared as a magazine serialisation, the reviews unanimously accused it of betraying its author's own immoral lifestyle. In 1895, the prosecuting council at Wilde's Old Bailey trial quoted the book at length during his cross-examination in an attempt to prove that Wilde was guilty of his leading character's crimes, chiefly that of practising homosexuality. Wilde himself encouraged this biographical reading. He famously said that Lord Henry was a portrayal of himself as the world thought him to be, but that Basil Hallward was how he saw himself. As ever, he was being creative with the truth. Lord Henry is perhaps a deeper portrait than his creator knew or intended. He may be fashionably paradoxical and superficial in both his conversation and daily life, but behind this verbal smokescreen he has a genuinely savage intellectual contempt for the bourgeois niceties and evasions of his society and (as he nears the end of his story) an almost tragic self-awareness that go way beyond the popular caricature of Wilde as an effete dandy and give us – with hindsight – perhaps the truest self-image of the great man himself outside of *De Profundis*. Basil, meanwhile, may share Wilde's own vulnerability to unrequited love for good-looking young men who cannot possibly either understand or reciprocate his devotion, but there the similarities tellingly end – or rather, stray into wish-fulfillment. Wilde never dared, as Basil does, to cut himself free from his infatuation, pack his bags and set out for Paris in order to dedicate himself entirely to his work (the very steps, not at all coincidentally, that several of Wilde's friends were to beg him to take in the twenty-four hours before his eventual arrest in 1895). Perhaps this act of moral and emotional courage was why Wilde saw fit to deprive Basil of his planned new life just twenty minutes before he starts it, and to finish him off with such a violent, horrible and curiously sexual death; he had to be punished for an erotic and emotional honesty of which his creator (and his century) were convinced they could only dream.

The oddest correspondence between Wilde's life and fiction comes in the character of Dorian himself. Like Lord Alfred Douglas, Dorian is blond-haired, blue-eyed and red-lipped; indeed, the very same hackneyed phrases used to describe the young Dorian in the novel reappear almost word for word in Wilde's letters describing Douglas to his friends. Like Dorian, Douglas was upper-class Oxonian charm incarnate. Like Dorian, once he was launched into London Society he turned out to have an insatiable appetite for both working-class sex and upper-class luxury, to be a consummate liar, and to have a truly psychopathic disregard for the consequences of his actions on those close to him. The match is perfect. *The Picture of Dorian Gray*, however, was published in 1890, and Wilde didn't meet his nemesis until the summer of 1891. Dorian is not a reflection of Wilde's life, but an uncanny anticipation of it. He may be a complete fiction, but for the man who created him he turned out to be horribly and inescapably real. One of the reasons the story is so powerful, perhaps, is that we now know it to be the work of a man exactly imagining his own private hell of erotic and moral destruction, but unaware that he is doing just that.

## *'The artist is the creator of beautiful things'*
### This Adaptation

The word 'adaptation' can hide a multitude of sins in the theatre, but this one is as true to its source as over thirty years of my reading, studying, staging and having imaginary conversations with Oscar Wilde can make it. While using the extended narrative structure of the 1891 book-length version of the story, I have in several key places used the phrasing of Wilde's original 1890 typescript of the story, which has only recently been published (in 2011, in a brilliant edition by Nicholas Frankel for the Harvard University Press). Several key sentences and passages in this typescript were significantly toned down before publication, first by Wilde's editors, and later by Wilde himself, and the original is a salutary reminder of how authentically shocking the story's first appearance must have been, with its almost-candid references to both homosexual and heterosexual passions. Aficionados of the *Collected Works* will easily spot the places where – inspired by and hopefully justified by Wilde's own relentless re-cycling of his own best lines from work to work – I have used sentences from other plays and prose works to convey in succinct dialogue what in the book is conveyed in more extended prose. But rest assured, it is all Wilde. For instance, the fragment of the letter which Dorian writes to Sybil, which some eagle-eared audience members will correctly remember is not actually quoted in the novel, is in fact a fragment of one of Wilde's own. The curt first line of the show, which may be a surprise to those familiar with the novel's gloriously orchestrated opening description of a lazy London summer's afternoon, is in fact the *last* line of the self-justifying introductory preface which Wilde added to the 1891 book version of his story after it had been so savagely reviewed. My biggest intervention is one I'll freely admit to, the replacement of the lacklustre Hetty

Morton with the Duchess of Monmouth as Dorian's final real affair (Hetty, I'm afraid, is the character in the book-length version of the story where the author's rush to bash out his word-count and get to the end is most plainly visible). Her words are quarried more or less literally out of several passages from the novel's last three chapters, but I was inspired to make her American not only by the vivid real-life examples of all the American heiresses who did indeed marry into the British peerage either side of Wilde's *fin de siècle*, but also (and more immediately) by the half-contemptuous, half-admiring chatter about those ladies that surfaces in several of Wilde's stories, and which memorably decorates the dialogue of the first act of *A Woman of No Importance*. I also (it must be admitted) wanted to give the actress playing Sybil Vane, who as the first of Dorian's victims necessarily dies rather early on in the evening, a good crack at the second act, and this time to escape alive.

The interpretation of the time scheme of the novel is my own. Wilde tells us that Dorian is twenty when the story begins, and a day short of thirty-eight when he kills Basil Hallward. How much time then elapses before Dorian's own death then concludes the story is never specified. Since the start of the story is set in his own contemporary 1890s London, and since the action of that story must logically take at the very least nearly twenty years, Wilde implies that his anti-hero lives on well into the twentieth century – a century which Wilde himself barely survived into, and which for his original readers lay far in the unknowable future. I have simply stretched that conceit, thus making Dorian's *ennui* as the years mount a much more serious matter. In this time scheme, Lady Monmouth will almost certainly (I hope) end up in Paris partying with Nancy Cunard. Dorian will attend the first night of Coward's *The Vortex* – and probably wonder what all the fuss is about – and as Lord Henry dies will then face the prospect of the long, low, dishonest decade of the 1930s with limitless money and absolutely no friends. By freeing him from the constraining and perhaps over-familiar frame of a purely Victorian costume drama, I hope this imagery helps him to live as not only Wilde's contemporary but also, implicitly, as ours.

A few final practical thoughts for anyone considering taking on this script themselves. This piece was written for an ensemble of seventeen actors, but I imagine could be done with one or two less. With the exception of Dorian himself, all of the actors double both as other parts and as members of the Chorus – when speaking in their function of the chorus, outside of the story, their lines are marked in the script **in bold**; when they are speaking both outside of the story and outside of their characters – in other words, in their own voices and accents – their lines are marked ***in italics***. The pace of the script assumes that the story is being told in a single, striking stage environment, one in which location is conjured through the use of sound and light rather than on a series of descriptive sets requiring time-consuming scene changes. If at all possible, there should be no walls or doors, so that a character can go from room to room or from Belgravia to Limehouse by taking a single step.

The staging of Dorian's death and the final restoration of the picture can be as much of a *coup de theatre* or as little of one as the circumstances and logic of the production demand. In the book, it is done with great economy – nothing is shown. In the theatre, however…

The costumes, I rather think, should be sensational.

**Neil Bartlett**
London and Dublin, 2012

*This adaptation was originally commissioned by the Abbey Theatre for the 2012 Dublin Theatre Festival and it was first performed on 27 September 2012 in a production created by the following Company:*

| | |
|---|---|
| *Adapted and Directed by* | Neil Bartlett |
| *Set and Costume Design* | Kandis Cook |
| *Lighting Design* | Chris Davey |
| *Sound Design* | Ivan Birthistle |
| | Vincent Doherty |
| *Additional Staging by* | Paul Kieve |
| *Fight Director* | Donal O'Farrell |
| *Assistant Director* | Oonagh Murphy |
| *Voice Director* | Andrea Ainsworth |
| *Company Stage Manager* | Tara Furlong |
| *Deputy Stage Manager* | Deirdre McClean |
| *Assistant Stage Manager* | Richie O'Sullivan |
| *Casting Director* | Kelly Phelan |
| *Additional Casting* | Siobhan Bracke |
| *Hair and Make-up* | Val Sherlock |
| *Photography* | Ros Kavanagh |
| *Graphic Design* | Zero – G |
| *Set Construction* | The Natural Construction Company |
| | Vincent Bell |
| *Frame Construction* | David Shakarian |
| *Sign Language Interpreter* | Amanda Coogan |
| *Audio Description* | Bríd Ní Ghruagáin |
| | Maureen Portsmouth |
| *Captioning* | Ruth McCreery |
| | Paula McRedmond |

*Special thanks to Brian Madigan of CRC Medical, Dennis Chadwick of BOC Gases Ireland, Joe Brennan and John Heffernan of Megaflash Technologies.*

*Audio described and captioned performances are provided by Arts and Disability Ireland with funding from the Arts Council / An Chomhairle Ealaíon.*

OSCAR WILDE

# THE PICTURE OF DORIAN GRAY

ADAPTED BY NEIL BARTLETT

## CAST (IN ORDER OF APPEARANCE)

| | |
|---|---|
| *Jane Brennan* | Lady Victoria Wotton |
| *Jasper Britton* | Lord Henry Wotton |
| *Gerard Byrne* | Francis |
| *Tom Canton* | Dorian Gray |
| *Aaron Heffernan* | Victor |
| *Bob Kelly* | James Vane |
| *Emmet Kirwan* | Footman |
| *Andrew Macklin* | Alan Campbell |
| *Charlotte McCurry* | Sybil Vane & Gladys, Duchess of Monmouth |
| *Frank McCusker* | Basil Hallward |
| *Lise Ann McLaughlin* | Lady Agatha Carlisle |
| *Bairbre Ní Chaoimh* | Mrs Erlynne |
| *Kate O'Toole* | Mrs Leaf |
| *Ben Reynolds* | Ensemble |
| *Michael Sheehan* | Footman |
| *Ali White* | Lady Ruxton |
| *Susannah de Wrixon* | Lady Narborough |

*All other parts are played by the Company.*
*There will be one interval of 20 minutes.*

# CREATIVE TEAM & CAST

## NEIL BARTLETT
### WRITER & DIRECTOR

NEIL BARTLETT WAS AN early member of Complicite, with whom he won a Perrier Award for *More Bigger Snacks Now* in 1985 and a founder member of GLORIA (1988–1998), with whom he created thirteen theatre pieces including *A Vision of Love Revealed in Sleep*, *Sarrasine*, *Night after Night*, *A Judgement in Stone* and *The Seven Sacraments of Nicolas Poussin*, staged in venues ranging from The Royal Court to Southwark Cathedral. From 1994 to 2005 he was Artistic Director of the Lyric Hammersmith, where he staged *Britten, Dickens, Genet, Kleist, Marivaux, Maugham, Molière, Rattigan* and *Shakespeare and Wilde* and collaborated with artists as diverse as Improbable and Robert Lepage. He received an OBE and an Olivier Nomination for Outstanding Theatrical Achievement for his work there. Since leaving the Lyric, his work at the Abbey Theatre includes *An Ideal Husband*, while he has also directed *Romeo and Juliet* and *Twelfth Night* (Royal Shakespeare Company), *The Maids, The Girl I Left Behind Me, For Alfonso* and *What Can You Do?* (Brighton Festival), *The Pianist, Everybody Loves A Winner* and *The Madness of Extraordinary Plan* (Manchester International Festival), *The Rake's Progress* and *The Turn of the Screw* (Aldeburgh Festival), *Dido, Queen of Carthage* and *Oliver Twist* (American Repertory Theatre, Boston), *Or You Could Kiss Me*, a collaboration with Handspring, the creators of *Warhorse* (National Theatre, London) and *The Queen of Spades* (Opera North). He is also an author and novelist. His first book, *Who Was That Man?*, a ground-breaking study of Wilde, was published in 1988. His third novel, *Skin Lane*, was long-listed for the Costa Award in 2006. His translations, adaptations and solo performance pieces, together with his play *In Extremis*, commissioned by the National Theatre in London to celebrate the centenary of Wilde's death in 2000, are all published by Oberon Books. His future projects include a new music-theatre piece for next year's Brighton Festival, created in collaboration with lighting designer Paule Constable. You can find out more about Neil's work, and contact him, at www.neil-bartlett.com.

## KANDIS COOK
### SET AND COSTUME DESIGNER

KANDIS HAS DESIGNED costumes and sets for theatre, ballet, opera and film. Her work at the Abbey Theatre includes *Tartuffe* and *Portia Coughlan*. She has also designed for the Royal Court Theatre, Lyric Hammersmith, Manchester Royal Exchange, Liverpool Everyman, the Royal Shakespeare Company and the Globe Theatre. Recent costume designs include *School for Scandal* (Barbican Theatre and Holland Theatre Festival co-production). Design for ballet includes Birmingham Royal Ballet, Royal London Ballet, Royal Danish Ballet, San Francisco Ballet, Cincinnati Ballet, Houston Ballet, Australian Ballet, Tokyo National Ballet and Les Grande Ballets Canadienne, Montreal. Design for opera includes Opera North, Staatsoper Hamburg and Theatre an der Wien, Aldeburgh Festival, Wexford Opera Festival, Hans Christian Andersen Centenary Gladsaxe Theatre Copenhagen and Music Theatre at Staatsoper Stuttgart. Film work includes costumes for *The Piano Tuner of Earthquakes* directed by the Brothers Quay. She is co-founder of Post-Operative Productions through which she co-directed with Nick Till, multi-disciplinary music theatre from 1997–2007. Her next design commission will be for the London Royal Ballet, February 2013.

## CHRIS DAVEY
### LIGHTING DESIGN

CHRIS'S PREVIOUS WORK at the Abbey Theatre includes *An Ideal Husband* and *Closer*, Irish Times Theatre Award nomination for Best Lighting 2000. Recent designs include *Shelley* (Shared Experience), *Waiting for Godot* (West Yorkshire Playhouse), *DruidMurphy* (World Tour), *Shoes* (Sadler's Wells), *Carlos Acosta Premieres* (London Coliseum) and *The Madness of an Extraordinary Plan* (Manchester International Festival). Other theatre work includes *Or You Could Kiss Me*, *Beyond the Horizon*, *Spring Storm*, *Harper Regan*, *The Seagull*, *The Pillars of the Community*, *A Dream Play*, *Iphiginia at Aulis*, *War and Peace*, *Baby Doll* and *The Colour of Justice* (National Theatre), *Twelfth Night*, *The Winter's Tale*, *Pericles*, *Cymbeline*, *Alice in Wonderland*, *Night of the Soul*, *Romeo and Juliet*, *A Midsummer Night's Dream*, *Everyman* (both also in New York), *A Month in the Country*, *Troilus and Cressida*, *The Comedy of Errors* (world tour), *Mysteria* and *Easter* (Royal Shakespeare Company). Opera work includes *Madame Butterfly* (Oslo), *Romeo et Juliette* (Opera Ireland), *Hippolyte et Aricie* (Nationale Reisopera Netherlands), *L'Arbore di Diana* (Valencia), *I Capuleti E I Montecchi* (Opera North, Melbourne and Sydney Opera House), *Skellig* (The Sage Gateshead), *Aida* (Houston), *Bird* of Night (Royal Opera House), *Bluebeard* (Bregenz), *Jephtha* (English National Opera, Welsh National Opera and Copenhagen), *The Magic Flute* (Welsh National Opera and eight seasons for Grange Park Opera), *The Rake's Progress* and *The Turn of the Screw* (Aldeburgh Festival) and *The Picture of Dorian Gray* (Monte Carlo). Chris has designed extensively for Shared Experience Theatre, Royal Court, Hampstead Theatre, Lyric Hammersmith, Royal Exchange Manchester, West Yorkshire Playhouse, Royal Lyceum Edinburgh and Birmingham Rep. Chris won the Theatre Management Association Best Lighting Design Award for *Dial M for Murder* (West Yorkshire Playhouse) and *Beyond the Horizon* (Royal and Derngate, Northampton).

Women, *The Beauty Queen of Leenane, Homeplace, Dancing at Lughnasa, Much Ado About Nothing, Shadow of a Gunman* and *True West* (Lyric Theatre), *The Field* (Lane Productions), *Laundry* (ANU Productions), *Freefall, Mud, Foley* and *Lolita* (The Corn Exchange), *All in the Timing* (Innis Theatre Company), *The Sanctuary Lamp* and *Honour* (b*spoke), *Dying City* and *Pentecost* (Rough Magic), *This Is Our Youth, Wedding Day at the Cro-Magnons', Roberto Zucco, This is Not a Life, Beckett's Ghosts, Shooting Gallery, Far Away* and *The Massacre @ Paris* (Bedrock Theatre Company), *Miss Julie* and *Blackbird* (Landmark), *Pineapple, Chatroom, All About Town* and *Wunderkind* (Calipo Theatre Company), *Ladies and Gents, God's Grace, Adrenalin* and *Slaughter* (Semper-Fi).

## IVAN BIRTHISTLE AND VINCENT DOHERTY
### SOUND DESIGN

VINCENT AND IVAN WORK TOGETHER on an ongoing collaborative basis. Previous work at the Abbey Theatre includes *No Escape, The Playboy of the Western World, Saved, Alice Trilogy* and *True West*. Other theatre work includes *It Only Ever Happens In The Movies* (National Youth Theatre), *The Great Goat Bubble, Tiny Plays For Ireland, End Of The Road, Big Ol' Piece Of Cake, Rank, Noah and the Tower Flower, The Gist of It, Monged* and *Tadgh Stray Wandered In* (Fishamble, The New Play Company), *Touch Me, Swimming With My Mother, As You Are / Faun* and *Boxes* (Cois Céim Dance Theatre), *Dockers, The Absence of*

## DONAL O'FARRELL
### FIGHT DIRECTOR

DONAL O'FARRELL'S WORK as a fight director at the Abbey Theatre includes *The Government Inspector, Lovers at Versailles, The Big House, Hamlet, Portia Coughlan, Chun na Fairraige Síos, Defender of the Faith, Purgatory, The Dandy Dolls, I Do Not Like Thee, Doctor Fell, The Shaughraun, The House of Bernarda Alba, Henry IV, The Sanctuary Lamp, The Morning after Optimism, A Whistle in the Dark, A Life, The Wake* and *The Honey Spike*. Other theatre work includes *Done Up Like a Kipper, Juno and the Paycock, Maria* (Wexford Festival Opera) and *The Field* (SFX Theatre). Donal has worked as a stunt co-ordinator on films including *Good Vibrations, Shadow Dancer, Citadel, Whole Lotta Sole, The Guard, My Brothers, Runway, Happy Ever Afters, Triage, Cracks, Daisy Chain, Becoming Jane, The Tiger's Tale, Mighty Celt, Ek Tha Tiger, Sanctuary, Flowers of Desire, Haywire, Zonad, P.S. I Love You* and *Lassie*. Television work as a stunt co-ordinator includes *Love/Hate, Single Handed* and *Raw* (RTÉ), *Neverland, Hidden, Primeval, George Gently, Treasure Island, Jack Taylor, Rásaí na Gaillimhe, Murphy's Law* and *Titanic: Blood and Steel*. Donal has also worked as a fight director for the Gaiety Theatre, SFX Theatre and Project Arts Centre.

## OONAGH MURPHY
ASSISTANT DIRECTOR

OONAGH IS THE RESIDENT ASSISTANT DIRECTOR at the Abbey Theatre, where she has worked on *Into the Woods, Alice in Funderland*, the *Tom Mac Intyre Celebration, The Government Inspector* and *Translations*. Recent directing credits include as part of Cork Midsummer Festival, *Measure for Measure in TEXT | Messages* (Project Arts Centre), *Do You Read Me?* (Smock Alley Theatre and ABSOLUT Fringe 2011), *I am a Home Bird [It's Very Hard]* (Project Arts Centre) and *SQUAT* by Louise Melinn at Solstice (Cork Midsummer Festival), originally presented as part of The Theatre Machine Turns You On: Volume II and developed as part of Project Brand New, *FAT* (Players Theatre), and *Ann and Barry: What Kind of Time Do You Call This?* (National College of Art and Design, ABSOLUT Fringe 2009 and 2010) and *Nineteeneightyfour* (Samuel Beckett Theatre). Oonagh also worked as production dramaturg for the work-in-development *The Blue Boy* with Brokentalkers (Ulster Bank Dublin Theatre Festival 2010). She is a graduate of the Bachelor in Drama and Theatre Studies at Trinity College where she is also a PhD candidate researching contemporary Irish theatre practice.

## JANE BRENNAN
LADY VICTORIA WOTTON

JANE'S PREVIOUS WORK at the Abbey Theatre includes *Perve, No Escape, Alice Trilogy*, Winner Irish Times Theatre Award for Best Actress 2007, *Bailegangaire, The Burial at Thebes, The House*, Irish Times Theatre Award nomination for Best Actress, *Dancing at Lughnasa, The Last Apache Reunion, The Crucible, Footfalls, A Crucial Week in the Life of a Grocer's Assistant, The Playboy of the Western World, The Secret Fall of Constance Wilde, The Wake, Saint Joan* and *The Rivals*. Other theatre work includes *Jane Eyre, Pygmalion* and *Not I* (Gate Theatre), *'Tis Pity She's a Whore, A Little Like Drowning, The Singular Life of Albert Nobbs* and *The Beauty Queen of Leenane* (Druid Theatre Company), *Splendour*, Irish Times Theatre Award nomination for Best Supporting Actress 2008 (Project Arts Centre), *Digging For Fire, Solemn Mass for a Full Moon in Summer* and *The Way of the World* (Rough Magic), *The Sugar Wife* (Rough Magic and Soho Theatre) and *Hamlet*

(Second Age Theatre Company). Jane co-founded b*spoke Theatre Company and with them she has also appeared in *Electra*, *Boston Marriage* and *Tejas Verdes*. Film and television work includes *Single Handed 2*, *Fair City* and *Love/Hate* (RTÉ), *The Tudors* (Showtime), *Veronica Guerin* (Touchstone Pictures), *Benedict Arnold* (Dark Eagle Productions), *Perrier's Bounty* (Parallel Films), *Death of a Superhero* (Bavaria Pictures), *Loving Miss Hatto* (BBC), *Attracta* (B.A.C. Films) and *Black Day at Blackrock* (Venus Three Productions).

## JASPER BRITTON

### LORD HENRY WOTTON

THIS IS JASPER'S DEBUT at the Abbey Theatre. Other theatre work includes *Taming Of The Shrew* (RSC, Washington D.C. and West End, London), *Marat/Sade* (Royal Shakespeare Company and Royal Shakespeare Theatre), *Plague Over England* (Finborough Theatre), *The Tempest* (Globe Theatre), *Japes* (Theatre Royal Haymarket), *Mother Adam* (Jermyn Street Theatre) and *Fram* (National Theatre, London). Film credits include *The New World* (Storyline Cinema), *Anonymous* (Columbia Pictures) and *Blood* (BBC Films).

## GERARD BYRNE

### FRANCIS

GERARD'S PREVIOUS WORK at the Abbey Theatre includes *Arrah-na-Pogue*, *Tarry Flynn*, *Observe the Sons of Ulster Marching Towards the Somme*, *Macbeth*, *Frauds*, *Blinded by the Light*, *Strange Occurrence on Ireland's Eye* and *The Shaughraun*. Other theatre work includes *Home*, *Buddleia*, *War*, *Brownbread*, *Studs* and *The Birdtable* (The Passion Machine Theatre Company), *Emma*, *Silas Marner* and *Esther Waters* (Storytellers Theatre Company), *The Carnival King* (Fishamble: The New Play Company), *The Pope and the Witch* (Red Kettle), *West Side Story* (Olympia Theatre), *Summerhouse* (Druid Theatre Company), *The Man with the Flower in his Mouth*, *Impressions of Vincent* (*Van Gogh*), *The Man in the Iron Mask* and *The Man Who Cared Too Much* (Project Arts Centre), *Trojan Women* (Smock Alley Theatre), *What's Left of the Flag* (Theatre Upstairs), which received an Irish Times Best New Play nomination and *Overtime* (New Theatre). Film and television work includes *Before I Sleep* and *Tupperware* (Brother Films), *Crush Proof* (Continent Film GmbH), *After Midnight* (Channel 4 Films), *The Truth About Claire* and *Fair City* (RTÉ), *The Snapper* (BBC Films) and *Noreen* (Domhnall Gleeson). He was actor/presenter of the documentary *A Matter of Life and Debt* (Radharc and RTÉ) and *Happy Birthday Oscar Wilde* (Mind the Gap Films). He has also performed in a number of radio plays for both RTÉ and BBC Radio 4, the most recent of which was *The Hit List*, written and directed by John Boorman. Gerard has also worked and toured extensively in the UK and Europe. He has worked in both the Edinburgh Fringe and Edinburgh International Festivals, the Bonner Biennale Festival in Germany and the l'Imaginaire Irlandais festival at Théâtre de l'Europe, Paris.

## TOM CANTON
### DORIAN GRAY

THIS IS TOM'S DEBUT at the Abbey Theatre. Other theatre work includes *The Pillowman* (National Theatre London Associate Production), *One Minute*, *Cymbeline*, *Chelsea Hotel*, *Last Orders* and *Divine Words* (RADA). Film work includes *Shitkicker* (DP Films). Tom recently graduated from the Royal Academy of Dramatic Art (RADA) in London and previously trained at the Miskin Theatre. This is Tom's professional theatrical debut.

## AARON HEFFERNAN
### VICTOR

THIS IS AARON'S DEBUT at the Abbey Theatre. Other theatre work includes *The Wonderful World of Dissocia*, *Tiny Dynamite*, *Tender Napalm*, *Andorra*, *The Importance of Being Earnest* and *The Happy Prince* (Samuel Beckett Theatre), *Oklahoma!* (Mill Theatre) and *Monster/Clock* (Smock Alley Theatre). Aaron has also performed in two sell-out runs with comedy sketch group *A Betrayal of the Penguins* and a sell-out run with the satirical musical comedy *Obama Mia* (Edinburgh Festival Fringe).

## BOB KELLY
### JAMES VANE

THIS IS BOB'S DEBUT at the Abbey Theatre. Other theatre work includes *The Country Girls* (Red Kettle), *The King of the Great Clock Tower* (Royal Ballet School, London), *Fulgurances* (Musée du Louvre), *At Swim Two Birds*, *The Poor Mouth*, Irish Times Theatre Award nomination for Best Supporting Actor, and *Rhinoceros* (Blue Raincoat Theatre Company) and *L'Écrivain Public* (Plateforme Théâtre). Film and television work includes *Breithe agus Bás* (Tile Film), *Withdrawal* (Phil Sheerin), *Without Words* (Brian Deane) and *America The Story of US* (History Channel). Bob is a member of Scratch That improv comedy group and is a graduate of the École Internationale de Théâtre Jacques Lecoq.

## EMMET KIRWAN
### FOOTMAN

EMMET'S PREVIOUS WORK at the Abbey Theatre includes *Alice in Funderland*. Other theatre work includes *Bogboy* (Tall Tales), *Chicane* and *Shay and Aisling's Story* (Gúna Nua), *In Real Time* (Brokentalkers), *Mushroom* (Project Arts Centre), *Monged* (Fishamble: The New Play Company) *No Messin' with the Monkeys* (The Ark Theatre), *Where He Lies* and *Lovers* (Island Theatre Company), *One* (Pan Pan), *Election Night* (Bewley's Cafe Theatre), *Alone It Stands* (Lane Productions), *The Indian Wants the Coombe* (Purple Hart TC), *Ladies and Gents* and *Another 24 Hours* (Semper Fi and Traverse Theatre), *Car Show 3* (The Corn Exchange and Barabbas), *Ugly Penguin Scenarios* and *The Madman and The Nun* (Crypt Arts Centre), *Rent* (Olympia Theatre) and *Buzzin to Bits* and *Pericles* (Project @ The Mint). Television and film work includes *Legend* and *The Big Bow Wow* (RTÉ 2), *The Silence* (BBC),

*The Take* (Sky One), *Two Hearts* (Calipo Films), *Dublin In Pieces* and *Shattered* (I–Wire Films), *Porcelain* (Inis Films), *The Boys and Girls from County Clare* (Metro-Goldwyn), *Inside I'm Dancing* (Universal Pictures) and *Ella Enchanted* (Miramax Films). Emmet is also a writer of television, radio and theatre. He wrote and played the title character in the RTÉ comedy *Sarah and Steve* (Accomplise Television). His play *Half 3 Heroes*, was commissioned by Dublin Youth Theatre and performed in Project Arts Centre. Emmet is a graduate of the Samuel Beckett Centre, Trinity College Dublin.

## ANDREW MACKLIN
ALAN CAMPBELL

ANDREW'S PREVIOUS WORK at the Abbey Theatre includes *Three Sisters*. Other theatre work includes *The Only True History of Lizzie Finn* (Southwark Playhouse), *Brighton* (Garter Lane Arts Centre), *Cinderella* and *The Beauty Queen of Leenane* (Watford Palace Theatre), *I'll Be The Devil* (Royal Shakespeare Company and Tricycle Theatre), *All Over Town* (Calipo Theatre Company), *The Irish Curse* (Dublin International Gay Theatre Festival), *24 Hour Plays: Lucy's Brief Guide to being Human* (Old Vic Theatre), *Cinderella* and *Jack and the Beanstalk* (Salisbury Playhouse), *The Cure at Troy* (Floodtide Theatre Company), *Much Ado About Nothing* (Bath Theatre Royal), *Don't Look Back* (dreamthinkspeak), *Markings* (Attic Theatre Company) and *A Passionate Woman* (Sonning Theatre). Television work includes *Fair City* (RTÉ). Radio

work includes *No Nightingales, No Snakes* (BBC Radio 4), *Soundscape* (Unique, The Production Company), *The Pilferers* (Red Kettle) and *In My Father's House* (WLR Radio). Andrew trained at Bristol Old Vic Theatre School.

## CHARLOTTE MCCURRY
SYBIL VANE & GLADYS,
DUCHESS OF MONMOUTH

THIS IS CHARLOTTE'S DEBUT at the Abbey Theatre. Other theatre work includes *Hedda* (Green Room), *Both Sides* (Ransom Productions), *The Jungle Book* and *The Crucible* (Lyric Theatre), *The Great Carmo!* (Cahoots), *The Haunting of Helena Blunden* (Big Telly), *The Famous Five* (Tabard Theatre), *Kitty and Damnation* (Lion and Unicorn) and *Jack and the Beanstalk* (GOH, Belfast). Television work includes *The Titanic Inquiry* and *Our William* (BBC Northern Ireland).

## FRANK MCCUSKER
BASIL HALLWARD

FRANK'S PREVIOUS WORK at the Abbey Theatre includes *The Last Days of a Reluctant Tyrant, Julius Caesar, Defender of the Faith*, Winner Irish Times Theatre Award for Best Supporting Actor 2004, *The Wild Duck, Communion, The Sanctuary Lamp, Translations, The House, The Tempest, The Importance of Being Earnest, She Stoops to Folly, As the Beast Sleeps, Observe the Sons of Ulster Marching Towards the Somme, The Adventures of Shay Mouse, The*

*Third Law of Motion*, *The Last Apache Reunion*, *The Playboy of the Western World*, Winner Helen Hayes Award, Washington D.C., *The Glass Menagerie*, *The Gentle Island* and *The Lower Depths*. Other theatre work includes *The Ugly One* (Royal Court), *Under the Black Flag* and *Coriolanus* (Globe Theatre), *The Shadow of a Gunman* (Tricycle Theatre), *Aristocrats* (Gate Theatre and Lincoln Center, New York) and *The Collection* (Gate Theatre), *Life Support* (Aldwych Theatre), *Torchlight*, *Laserbeams* and *Equus* (Gaiety Theatre), *Wild Harvest* (Druid Theatre Company), *Moonshine* (Red Kettle) and *Hamlet* and *King Lear* (Second Age Theatre Company). Film and television work includes *The Railway Station Man* and *The Fall* (BBC), *David Copperfield* (Hallmark Entertainment), *Rebel Heart*, *As the Beast Sleeps* and *Pulling Moves* (BBC Northern Ireland), *The Affair of the Necklace* (Alcon Entertainment), *The Blackwater Lightship* (Gillham Road Productions), *Murder Prevention* (World Productions), *Bad Girls* (Shed Productions), *Hunger* (Film 4), *Circle of Friends* (Price Entertainment), *The Ambassador* (Ecosse Films), *Anytime Now* (Comet Productions), *Proof* (RTÉ), *Bitter Sweet* (Element Pictures), *Titanic: Blood and Steel* (Antena 3 Films), *The Tudors* (Showtime) and *1916 Seachtar Anaithnid* (Abu Media Films).

## LISE ANN MCLAUGHLIN
LADY AGATHA CARLISLE

LISE ANN'S PREVIOUS WORK at the Abbey Theatre includes *The Last Apache*

*Reunion*, *Nightshade*, *A Life*, *City Sugar*, *A Midsummer Night's Dream*, *Tainbocu*, *Ivanov*, *Stephen D*, *Wild Oats*, *The Star Turns Red* and *Mr Yeats and the Death of Cuchulain*. Other theatre work includes *Little Women*, *The Importance of Being Earnest* and *You Never Can Tell* (Gate Theatre), *Electra* (b*spoke Theatre Company), *Mums the Word*, *Candida*, *The Strangeness of Others* and *Stagestruck* (Wolsey Theatre, Ipswich), *Ourselves Alone* (Liverpool Playhouse and Royal Court Theatre) and *Una Pooka* (Tricycle Theatre). Film and television work includes *The Irish RM*, *Angel*, *Malice Aforethought*, *The Return* and *Whistleblower* (Channel 4), *Vexed*, *Thirteen Steps Down*, *Friends and Other Lovers*, *We'll Meet Again* (TV Times Award for Best Newcomer) and *Square Deal* (ITV), *Fair City*, *Teresa's Wedding*, *Miracles and Miss Langan* and *A Life* (RTÉ) and *Nobody's Property*, *Katie the Year of a Child*, *Dead Entry*, *Haggard*, *Yo Picasso*, *Easter 2016*, *Ties of Blood* and *Shadows on our Skin* (BBC).

## BAIRBRE NÍ CHAOIMH
MRS ERLYNNE

BAIRBRE'S PREVIOUS WORK at the Abbey Theatre includes *The Life of Galileo*, *The King of Friday's Men*, *The Sanctuary Lamp*, *Drama at Inish*, *The Far Off Hills*, *Candide*, *Ulysses in Night-Town*, *Deoraíocht*, *Scéal Scéalaí* and *Cúirt an Mheanoíche*. She was an Associate Artist at the Abbey from 2005–2008. Other theatre work includes *Private Lives*, *A Midsummer Night's Dream*, *The Rivals*, *Salomé* and *Come and Go* (Gate Theatre),

*The Shaughraun* and *The Playboy of the Western World* (Druid Theatre Company), *The Whisperers* and *I Can't Get Started* (Rough Magic), *Othello* (The London Stage Company tour of Japan), *Legends, Women in Arms* and *Wuthering Heights* (Storytellers), *Farawayan* and *Hughie on the Wires* (Calypso), *Romeo and Juliet* (Second Age Theatre Company), *The Glass Menagerie, Who's Afraid of Virginia Wolf, A Place With The Pigs* and *Lovers* (Focus Theatre), *Fear An Tae* (Amharclann de h-Íde), *An Triail* (Aisling Ghéar), *The Stronger, Dinner in Mulberry Street* and *Village Wooing* (Bewley's Café Theatre). She acted in several site-specific pieces including *Basin* and *Laundry*, Winner Irish Times Theatre Award for Best Production 2011 (ANU Productions), *Hand Me Down The Moon* (Women in Space) and *The End of the Road* (Fishamble: The New Play Company). Film and television work includes *Washed Up Love* (Jumper Productions), *Les Poneys Sauvages* (TFI), *Angela's Ashes* (Paramount Pictures), *Falling for a Dancer* (Parallel Films), *Frankie Starlight* (Ferndale Films), *The Fantasist* (Forstarter Productions), *Rawhead Rex* (Paradise Pictures), *Val Falvey, Lovers of The Lake, Fair City, Friends for Life, Hamlet and Her Brothers, Caught in A Free State, Glenroe* and *Finbar's Class* (RTÉ), *August Saturday* and *Aristocrats* (BBC), *The Real Charlotte* (Granada), *The Irish RM, The Playboy of the Western World* and *The Outcasts* (Channel 4) and *Corp Agus Anam, Paddywhackery, Aifric* and *Na Fíorghaeil* (TG4). Bairbre also works as a theatre director. She directed the multi-award winning *Catalpa* and *Play, Come And Go* and *Act Without*

Words II* for the Gate Theatre and received an Irish Times Theatre Award for her work with Calypso Productions.

## KATE O'TOOLE
MRS LEAF

KATE'S PREVIOUS WORK at the Abbey Theatre includes *The Barbaric Comedies* and *Drama at Inish*. Other theatre work includes *The Hostage* (Irish Arts Centre, New York), *John Bull's Other Island* (Gaiety Theatre), *Double Cross* (Field Day Theatre Company), *Reflected Glory* (Vaudeville, London), *Summer and Smoke* (Apollo Theatre, London), *The Blue Macushla, A Little Like Drowning* and *The Donahue Sisters* (Druid Theatre Company), *The House of Bernarda Alba* (Gate Theatre), *Macbeth* (Second Age Theatre Company), *Dancing at Lughnasa* (An Grianán), *Candida* (Heritage Theatre, New York), *Vanderbilts* (Hyde Park Theatre Festival, New York), *Don Juan* (Royal Exchange, Manchester), *The Provok'd Wife* (The National, London), *Dead Funny*, Irish Times Theatre Award nomination for Best Actress (Rough Magic) and *Three Tall Women*, Barclay's UK Award for Best Actress (Lyric Theatre). Television work includes *My Phone Genie, Glenroe* and *Proof* (RTÉ), *No Tears* (RTÉ and Comet Films), *Karaoke, Malice Afterthought, The Tudors, Titanic: Blood and Steel, Man on the Train, Laughter in the Dark, Dancing at Lughnasa, Eden, 32a, Javelina, The Ballad of Des and Mo'* and *The Dead*. Kate produced a short film, *Good Luck Mr. Gorski*, which won the People's Choice Award at the Taos Shortz Film Festival

2011. Kate is Chairwoman of the Board for the Galway Film Fleadh.

## BEN REYNOLDS
ENSEMBLE

THIS IS BEN'S DEBUT at the Abbey Theatre. Other theatre work includes *Jesus Caesar* (Company D), *Love Songs For Losers* (Absolut Fringe 2011), *Bang Shoot Blast* and *Other People's Stuff* (Come As Soon As You Hear), *The Quare Fellow* (The New Theatre), *Sive* (Trinity College Dublin Players) and *Sonnets For An Old Century* (Independent Youth Theatre). Television work includes *Ceart Agus Coir* (TG4).

## MICHAEL SHEEHAN
FOOTMAN

THIS IS MICHAEL'S DEBUT at the Abbey Theatre. Other theatre work includes *Fight Night* (Tron Theatre Glasgow), *Alone It Stands* (Lane Productions), *Way To Heaven* (Gallowglass) and *Titus Andronicus* (Siren Productions). Film and television work includes *The Consolation of Orion* (El Zorrero Films), *Hate* (I–Wire Films), *Insatiable* (Kirby Films) and *Fair City, The Clinic, Naked Camera* and *Prosperity* (RTÉ). Michael trained at The Gaiety School of Acting.

## ALI WHITE
LADY RUXTON

ALI'S PREVIOUS WORK at the Abbey Theatre includes *The Passing, Romeo and Juliet, Closer, The House, Dancing at Lughnasa, Translations, Philadelphia, Here I Come!* and *The Trojan Women.* Other theatre work includes *The School for Scandal, Spokesong, Northern Star, Is This About Sex?, Plaza Suite, Lady Windermere's Fan* and *Love and a Bottle* (Rough Magic), *Aristocrats, The Double Dealer, Catastrophe, Come and Go, Play* and *A Midsummer Night's Dream* (Gate Theatre), *Love and Money* (HATCH Theatre Company), *This Is What We Sang* (Kabosh Theatre Company), *Faith Healer* (Town Hall Galway), *Silas Marner* and *Hard Times* (Storytellers Theatre Company), *Cheapside* (Druid Theatre Company), *Factory Girls* (Bickerstaffe), *The Steward of Christendom* (Out of Joint), *The Silver Tassie* (Almeida), *Pygmies in the Ruins* (The Royal Court), *The Importance of Being Earnest* (The West Yorkshire Playhouse) and *Playhouse Creatures* (The Old Vic). Film and television work includes *No Tears, When Brendan Met Trudy* and *A Love Divided* (Parallel Films), *With or Without You* (Revolution Films), *The Ambassador* (BBC) and *Flush* (Flush Films). Radio work includes productions with RTÉ Radio Drama and BBC Radio Ulster. Ali also wrote and co-created *Any Time Now* (RTÉ and BBC) and worked as a screenwriter on *The Clinic* (Parallel Films). Her radio play *The Fly in the Cathedral* was produced by BBC Radio 4.

## SUSANNAH DE WRIXON
LADY NARBOROUGH

SUSANNAH'S PREVIOUS WORK at
the Abbey Theatre includes *Alice in
Funderland*, *Pygmalion*, *The Comedy
of Errors*, *An Ideal Husband*, *The
Shaughraun*, *Living Quarters* and
*Saint Joan*. Other theatre work includes
*Dancing at Lughnasa* (Second Age
Theatre Company), *Fewer Emergencies*
(Project Arts Centre), *I, Keano* (Olympia
Theatre), *Just a Little One* (Bewley's Café
Theatre and Kilkenny Arts Festival),
*As Married as We Get* (Bewley's Café
Theatre), *Annie* (Tivoli Theatre),
*Julius Caesar, Measure for Measure,
Coriolanus* and *The Revenger's Tragedy*
(Loose Canon) and *Car Show* (The Corn
Exchange). Film and television credits
include *Une Épopée*, *The Clinic*, *Fair
City* and *Ballykissangel*. As a singer
Susannah performed in *Adolf Gabler* a
piece by Roger Doyle with the National
Symphony Orchestra, *The Alternative
American Songbook* (National Concert
Hall), *Blossom...dearly* and *Away in
A Major* (Irish tour), *Fever* (Irish and
US tour), *Please Don't Make Me Feel So
Happy* (Olympia Theatre), *The Girls
of Summer* (Opera Theatre Company),
*Kurt Weill Kaberet* and *Farewell Ella*
(Andrews Lane Theatre) and *Pyjama Jazz*
(Tivoli Theatre). Susannah was one of *The
Nualas* trio. She has also recorded three
albums *Pick Yourself Up*, *She Swims in
the Sea* and *Tiny Tunes for Tiny People*.
Susannah trained at the Samuel Beckett
Centre, Trinity College Dublin.

THE PICTURE OF DORIAN GRAY

Oscar Wilde's

# THE PICTURE OF DORIAN GRAY

Adapted by Neil Bartlett

OBERON BOOKS
LONDON

WWW.OBERONBOOKS.COM

First published in 2012 by Oberon Books Ltd
521 Caledonian Road, London N7 9RH
Tel: +44 (0) 20 7607 3637 / Fax: +44 (0) 20 7607 3629
e-mail: info@oberonbooks.com
www.oberonbooks.com

A catalogue record for this book is available from the British Library.

PB ISBN: 978-1-84943-454-6
E ISBN: 978-1-84943-681-6

Cover: Photography by Ros Kavanagh
Design by Zero-G

Printed, bound and converted
by CPI Group (UK) Ltd, Croydon, CR0 4YY.

Visit www.oberonbooks.com to read more about all our books
and to buy them. You will also find features, author interviews and
news of any author events, and you can sign up for e-newsletters
so that you're always first to hear about our new releases.

# A PROLOGUE

*The traffic noise of London recedes into a distant roar.*

*A  group of people are looking at a painted canvas on an easel. It is a black, light-absorbing blank.*

*Two figures; LORD HENRY WOTTON and BASIL HALLWARD. BASIL is posed as if working on a painting. LORD HENRY is looking at the painting. They look like waxworks. An empty posing platform; a bowl of white lilacs.*

*Two handsome young FOOTMEN lounge provocatively.*

*FRANCIS enters. He takes a gold cigarette case out of his breast pocket, takes out a cigarette and lights it.*

FRANCIS: ***All Art Is Quite Useless.***

> *He dismisses the assembled crowd.*

> ***Thank you.***

> *MRS LEAF emerges from the shadows to assist in the preparations. FRANCIS places his burning cigarette in LORD HENRY's waiting fingers; MRS LEAF places a palette knife in BASIL's. The gold cigarette case is set ready for LORD HENRY's use.*

> *When all is ready to his satisfaction, FRANCIS formally begins the scene.*

> ***Thank you.***

> *An ormolu clock strikes three – and the tableau comes to life.*

> *FRANCIS retires and waits.*

# ACT ONE

## SCENE ONE
### BASIL HALLWARD'S STUDIO, HOLLAND PARK. SUMMER

LORD HENRY: It is your best work, Basil; the best thing you have ever done. You must certainly send it next year to the Grosvenor. The Academy is too large and too vulgar – whenever I have gone there, there have been either so many people that I have not been able to see the pictures, which was dreadful, or so many pictures that I have not been able to see the people, which was worse. The Grosvenor is really the only place.

BASIL: *(Working.)* I don't think I shall send it anywhere.

LORD HENRY: Not send it anywhere? My dear fellow, why? A portrait like this would set you far above all the young men in England, and make the old men quite jealous. If old men are capable of feeling any emotion.

BASIL: I have put too much of myself into it.

LORD HENRY: Too much of yourself! I never knew you were so vain… I really can't see any likeness between you and this young *(He is about to say something obscene.)* …this young Adonis of yours. Who's name, by the way, you have never told me.

BASIL: Of course I don't look like him…and I should be sorry to. There's a sort of fatality about distinction, don't you think? – the ugly and the stupid always have the best of it. Your rank and wealth Harry, my brains – my art, whatever it may be worth – Dorian Gray's good looks…we will all suffer terribly for what the gods have given us. Suffer. Terribly.

LORD HENRY: Dorian Gray. Is that his name?

*BASIL stops working, realising what he has just done.*

BASIL: Yes; that is his name. I didn't intend to tell it to you.

LORD HENRY: And why not?

BASIL: Oh… You know how I love secrecy. It seems to be the one thing that can make modern life mysterious or marvellous. Whenever I leave town now, I never tell my people where I'm going – a silly habit, but at least it brings a little romance into one's life. I suppose you think that foolish.

LORD HENRY: Not at all…not at all, my dear Basil; you seem to forget that I am married, and the one charm of marriage is that it makes a life of deception necessary for both parties. I never know where my wife is, and my wife never knows what I am doing. When we do meet, we tell each other the most absurd stories… She's very good at it – much better than I am. She never gets confused over her dates.

BASIL: *(Wiping his brushes; a pause in the work.)* I believe you're really a very good husband, Harry. Your cynicism is simply a pose.

LORD HENRY: Being natural is simply a pose, Basil – and the most irritating pose I know.

*A tricky moment; then they laugh.*

I should go, I'm meeting a man at the Curzon – but before I do, I insist on your answering my question.

BASIL: What question?

LORD HENRY: You know quite well.

BASIL: I don't.

LORD HENRY: I want you to explain to me the reason why you won't exhibit Dorian Gray's picture. I want the real reason.

BASIL: I told you the real reason.

LORD HENRY: No, you did not.

*A beat. MRS LEAF listens intently.*

BASIL: The reason I will not exhibit this picture is that I am afraid that I have shown in it the secret of my own soul.

LORD HENRY: Your *soul?* I am all expectation, Basil.

BASIL: Oh there is really very little to tell – and I am afraid you will hardly understand it. Or even perhaps believe it.

LORD HENRY: I am quite sure I shall understand it. And as for believing things, I can believe anything, provided that it is quite incredible.

BASIL: Well, this is. To me. At times.

The story is simply this; two months ago, I went to a crush at Lady Brandon's –

LORD HENRY: Ah! Lady Brandon… –

BASIL: Harry –

LORD HENRY: My dear fellow, she tried to found a salon, and only succeeded in opening a restaurant; how could I like her? Do go on.

BASIL: I was determined to only stay ten minutes – oh, you know the kind of thing –

FRANCIS: ***Over-dressed dowagers; stockbrokers in white tie trying to gain a reputation for being civilised –***

BASIL: but then I became aware that someone was looking at me. I turned half-way round…and saw Dorian Gray for the first time.

*Perhaps we hear a warped echo of the chatter of a society party; the lighting subtly distorts…*

*A pause.*

LORD HENRY: Yes.

MRS LEAF: ***Yes?***

BASIL: It was furiously hot, and… We were quite close, almost touching. When our eyes met, a curious sensation, a curious sensation of *terror* came over me. You know, Harry, I have always been my own master – had at least always been so, till I met Dorian. I tried to leave the room, from a sort of cowardice I suppose, but Lady Brandon seized me and insisted on making introductions. In that curiously shrill voice of hers, you know –

MRS LEAF MIMICKING LADY BRANDON: *"Not running away, Mr. Hallward?"*

LORD HENRY: Dear Lady Brandon. A peacock in everything but beauty. And what did she have to say about your wonderful young man?

*BASIL and MRS LEAF speak simultaneously;*

BASIL: Oh something about him being charming – "Poor dear mother and I absolutely inseparable. Quite forget what he does – afraid he doesn't do anything – oh yes, plays the piano – or is it the violin Mr Gray?"

MRS LEAF AS LADY BRANDON: *"Poor dear mother and I absolutely inseparable. Quite forget what he does – afraid he doesn't do anything – oh yes, plays the piano – or is it the violin Mr. Gray?"*

*In a burst of laughter, the party and the lights fade away.*

BASIL: Neither of us could help laughing, and we became friends at once.

LORD HENRY: Laughter is not at all a bad beginning for a friendship, and it is far the best ending for one. How often do you see him?

*A pause.*

MRS. LEAF: *Every day.*

BASIL: Every day. I couldn't be happy if I didn't see him every day.

LORD HENRY: How English you are, Basil. And is he very fond of you?

BASIL: I know he likes me. Of course I flatter him dreadfully… *(Suddenly breaking.)* Harry I feel as if I have given my whole soul away to someone who treats it as if it were a flower to put in his coat, an ornament for a summer's day.

LORD HENRY: Days in summer, Basil, are apt to linger.

*Music; a Chopin prelude. DORIAN is playing the piano in the other room.*

BASIL: I don't want you to meet him.

LORD HENRY: You don't want me to meet him?

BASIL: No. Harry, the world is wide, and full of marvellous people; please don't take away from me the one person who has given my life and my work whatever meaning it might possess. You mustn't try and –

FRANCIS: **Mr Dorian Gray, sir.**

LORD HENRY: You'll have to introduce me now.

*As he enters, DORIAN is reading the sheet-music of the Chopin. He emerges from darkness – in other words, he seems to come from nowhere. He is of extraordinary charm and beauty – all the more extraordinary because he seems to have no idea of the impact he has on people.*

DORIAN: Basil, you must lend me these, they are perfectly charming – oh I beg your pardon, I didn't know you had anyone with you.

LORD HENRY: Yes, they are. Whenever I hear Chopin, I always feel I should be weeping over sins I have not yet committed.

BASIL: Dorian, meet Lord Henry Wotton – an old Oxford friend of mine, and a bad influence on everyone he meets. We have just been discussing your picture.

DORIAN: Oh that. Lord Henry.

*He offers LORD HENRY his hand. Slightly gauche; but Oxonian charm incarnate.*

LORD HENRY: Mr. Gray.

DORIAN: I think we both know Lady Carlisle.

LORD HENRY: Do we?

*LORD HENRY looks at DORIAN's hand but does not shake it.*

DORIAN: I'm one of her "favourites" – I mean, we play duets together on her Tuesdays sometimes, at her charity down in Whitechapel. I do it as a sort of penance I suppose.

LORD HENRY: But you are far too charming to go in for Philanthropy, Mr Gray – far too charming. *(Offering him a cigarette from the gold cigarette case.)* Cigarette?

DORIAN: Thank you.

BASIL: Harry, would you think it awfully rude if I asked you to go away?

LORD HENRY: Why?

BASIL: Because I rather want to finish this today. Dorian – shall we?

DORIAN: I suppose so.

*Quite un-selfconsciously, DORIAN goes behind a screen and starts to change into the clothes required for the portrait. PARKER assists.*

LORD HENRY: Am I to go, Mr Gray?

DORIAN: *(Behind the screen.)* Oh please don't. It's horribly dull standing on a platform trying to look pleasant – especially when Basil is in one of his sulky moods. I'm sure I'll do better with someone to chat to. You can tell me why you think I shouldn't go in for Philanthropy.

LORD HENRY: I don't know that I could do that, Mr Gray; it is so tedious a subject one would have to talk seriously about it.

DORIAN: *(Laughing behind the screen.)* You don't mind really do you Basil? Oh come on, do ask him to stay.

BASIL: Harry, please stay. It's quite true I never talk when I'm working. *(Making a joke of it.)* And I never listen either! Which I advise you not to do!

*DORIAN appears. Dazzling.*

BASIL: Thank you… Chin up!

*DORIAN gets up on the podium. BASIL paints. LORD HENRY stops staring, and considers… Silence.*

DORIAN: Have you really a very bad influence, Lord Henry?

BASIL: Head to the left.

LORD HENRY: There is no such thing as a good influence, Mr Gray. All influence is immoral.

DORIAN: Why?

BASIL: Dorian! Thank you.

LORD HENRY: Because to influence a person is to give him one's own soul.

He does not think his natural thoughts, or burn with his natural passions. His virtues are not real to him. His sins, if there are such things as sins, are borrowed. He becomes an echo of someone else's music, an actor of a part that has not been written for him… The aim of life is self-development, Mr Gray; to realise one's nature perfectly – that is what each of us is here for. People are afraid of themselves, nowadays – they are charitable, they feed the hungry and clothe the beggar, but they have forgotten the highest of all duties, the duty that one owes to one's self. The terror of society, which is the basis of morals, and the terror of God, which is the basis of religion – these are the two things that govern us. Still. And yet – head just to the left, Mr Gray, there's a good boy – I believe that if one man were to live out his life fully and completely, were to give form to every feeling, expression to every thought, reality to every dream, the world would gain such an impulse of *joy*…

*The Chopin music creeps back into DORIAN's mind – but strangely distorted.*

But the bravest amongst us is afraid of himself. We are punished for our refusals, of course. Every impulse that we strive to strangle broods in the mind, and poisons us. The only way to get rid of a temptation is to yield to it. Resist it, and your soul grows sick with longing for the things it has forbidden itself, with desire for what its monstrous laws have made monstrous and unlawful… It is in the brain, and the brain only, that the great sins of the world take place. You, Mr Gray – you yourself, with your rose-red youth and your rose-white boyhood, you have had passions that have made you afraid…

Passions that have made you afraid; thoughts that have filled you with terror; day dreams and sleeping dreams whose mere memory might stain your cheeks with shame –

*The music abruptly vanishes, as;*

DORIAN: *(Breaking his pose.)* Stop! Can we stop for a moment? Sorry. I just need to…I just need to think.

BASIL: *(Still intent on his work.)* Harry, what have you been saying to him…?

LORD HENRY: Words; mere words. But then, is there anything so real? So vivid. So cruel…

DORIAN: Basil, do you think I might have something to drink? It really is stifling in here.

BASIL: I'm so sorry – hang on –

*BASIL rings for PARKER – never once taking his eyes off his work, working fast and fluently with a palette knife –*

Why don't you go out and sit in the garden – I've nearly got the effect I wanted but I need to work up this background a bit. I've no idea what Harry has been saying to you, but he's given you the most wonderful expression. I suppose he's been paying you compliments. You mustn't believe a word he says.

DORIAN: I don't.

*DORIAN escapes out into the air of the garden.*

*PARKER has entered; FRANCIS checks his appearance.*

PARKER: Sir.

BASIL: Something with ice in it please Parker.

PARKER: Sir.

LORD HENRY: And strawberries.

PARKER: My Lord.

*PARKER fetches the drinks. BASIL paints. LORD HENRY considers the effect he has had on DORIAN. He joins him in the garden.*

LORD HENRY: You know you believe it all.

*The iced drinks arrive.*

FRANCIS: *(From inside.)* Thank you Parker!

*Half way through his exit PARKER stops, and joins FRANCIS and MRS LEAF in the role of witness.*

*DORIAN gulps down the iced drink.*

LORD HENRY: You are quite right to do that. Nothing can cure the soul but the senses – just as nothing can cure the senses but the soul.

You know more than you think you know. Don't you.

DORIAN: Lord Henry –

LORD HENRY: It is absurd of you to be frightened. You are not a schoolboy, or a girl…and do come and sit here in the shade – if you stay any longer in that glare you will be quite spoiled, and Basil will never paint you again. You really must not allow yourself to become sunburnt. It would be very unbecoming.

DORIAN: What could that matter?

LORD HENRY: It should matter everything – to you, Mr Gray.

DORIAN: Why?

LORD HENRY: Because you have the most marvellous youth, and youth is the one thing worth having.

DORIAN: I don't feel that.

LORD HENRY: No, you don't feel it, *now.* But when you are old and wrinkled you will feel it terribly. You have a wonderfully beautiful face, Mr Gray – don't frown, you have – and wherever you go, I am sure you charm the world; but when your youth goes, your beauty will go with it, and then you will suddenly discover that there are no triumphs left. What the gods give, they take quickly away. The laburnam will be as yellow next June as it is now; in a month there will be purple flowers on the clematis, and year after year the green night of its leaves will hold its purple flowers – but we never get back our youth. Don't squander the gold of your days listening to the tedious or trying to improve the ignorant; live! Live the wonderful life that is in you. Realise your youth. Let nothing be lost upon you. Be afraid of *nothing...*

*BASIL is standing in the doorway, watching them.*

LORD HENRY: You are glad you have met me, Mr Gray.

DORIAN: Yes, I am. I wonder, shall I always be?

LORD HENRY: Always. That is a dreadful word.

BASIL: It's finished.

DORIAN: What is?

BASIL: The picture. It's quite finished.

*PARKER, MRS LEAF and FRANCIS all go subtly onto alert; they know what is coming.*

*LORD HENRY goes to look at the picture; DORIAN holds back.*

LORD HENRY: It is the finest portrait of our times. Congratulations.

Mr Gray, come and look at yourself.

BASIL: You sat wonderfully today – thank you.

LORD HENRY: Ah, that is entirely due to me – isn't it, Mr Gray?

*DORIAN looks at the picture; he recoils in shock. The Chorus amplifies his breath –*

**PARKER, FRANCIS, MRS LEAF: *Ah!***

**FRANCIS: *He had never really felt it before. His beauty – but now...***

**MRS LEAF: *Ah; now –***

**PARKER: *– His amethyst eyes deepened in a mist of tears.***

**MRS LEAF**: *(Viciously.) **As if he recognised himself for the very first time...***

BASIL: Well? Don't you like it?

LORD HENRY: Of course he likes it – it is one of the greatest things in modern art. I will give you anything you care to ask for it.

BASIL: The painting belongs to Dorian.

LORD HENRY: Then he's a very lucky fellow.

DORIAN: I think it's rather sad. I shall grow old and dreadful and uncouth, but this picture will never be older than this particular day in June. If only it were the other way.

BASIL: What do you mean?

DORIAN: If only it were I who was always to be young, and your picture that was to grow old. For that – for that I would give everything. Everything in the world. I think I would give my soul.

*DORIAN makes his pact with the devil with no consciousness at all of what it means – he is tired, emotional, confused, aroused – and twenty. But the members of the chorus know what he has just done… MRS. LEAF, FRANCIS and PARKER cross themselves.*

LORD HENRY: You would hardly care for such an arrangement, Basil. It would be rather hard lines on your work.

BASIL: *(Almost laughing.)* I should object very strongly, Harry.

DORIAN: *(Turning on him.)* Perhaps because you like your art better than you like your friends. And how long *will* I be your friend, Basil – till I have my first wrinkle, I suppose. Lord Wotton is right; youth is the only thing worth having. When I find that I am growing old, I shall kill myself.

BASIL: You're not jealous, are you?

DORIAN: I am jealous of everything whose beauty does not die. I am jealous of your portrait. Why should it keep what I must lose? In fact, why did you paint it?

*DORIAN turns away to try and stop himself from crying. A very awkward silence.*

BASIL: *(Furious, sotto voce.)* This is your doing, Harry.

LORD HENRY: *(Fascinated.)* "This" is the real Dorian Gray, that is all.

BASIL: It is not.

LORD HENRY: If it is not, what have I to do with it?

*BASIL is distraught that he has made DORIAN cry.*

MRS. LEAF (FRANCIS and PARKER *sotto voce*): **That knife looks sharp.**

*BASIL picks up the palette knife.*

BASIL: I'll destroy it.

*BASIL goes to slash the canvas; DORIAN stops him – a violent tussle.*

DORIAN: No!! Don't, Basil – don't! It would be murder.

BASIL: I am so glad you appreciate my work at last.

DORIAN: Appreciate it? I am in love with it. It's part of myself.

BASIL: Well, as soon as you are dry, you shall be varnished and framed, and sent home. Then you can do what you like with yourself.

*BASIL takes a deep breath, and attempts to restore normality.*

How about some tea. Harry? Or do you object to such simple pleasures?

*BASIL rings; PARKER brings tea.*

LORD HENRY: I adore simple pleasures. They are the last refuge of the complex. But I don't like scenes…except on stage. What silly boys you both are to squabble over a picture.

DORIAN: I don't allow people to call me a boy.

LORD HENRY: I'm sure you don't…

BASIL: Thank you Parker.

LORD HENRY: Let us go to the theatre tonight. There is bound to be something on, somewhere.

BASIL: Oh Harry –

*Under this next dialogue, the footlights begin to glow. We hear the murmur of an audience – at the nod from FRANCIS, PARKER and the FOOTMEN begin to re-arrange some gilt chairs to create the next scene.*

LORD HENRY: I had promised to dine at White's, but only with an old friend – I shall wire to say that I am prevented from coming in consequence of a subsequent engagement. It will have all the surprise of candour.

BASIL: It's such a bore putting on one's dress-clothes. And when one has them on, they're so horrid.

LORD HENRY: Yes, the costume of the century is detestable. Sin is the only colour-element left in modern life.

*DORIAN laughs – and we hear canned laughter – as if at a laugh-line in an Oscar Wilde play. BASIL is furious with LORD HENRY's (conspicuously successful) attempts to impress DORIAN.*

BASIL: You really mustn't say things like that before Dorian, Harry.

LORD HENRY: Before which Dorian? The one who is pouring out my tea, or the one in the picture?

*Laughter. Members of an 1895 West End theatre audience begin to drift surreally onto the stage – gowns, fans, programmes.*

DORIAN: *(With decision.)* I should adore to come to the theatre with you, Lord Henry.

LORD HENRY: Then you shall.

BASIL: I thought you might stop and dine with me.

DORIAN: I can't.

BASIL: Why?

DORIAN: Because I have promised Lord Henry to go with him.

*Laughter.*

BASIL: He won't like you any better for keeping your promises. He always breaks his.

*Laughter.*

DORIAN: Basil!… I must.

BASIL: Oh all right… Come and see me tomorrow.

DORIAN: Of course. Parker, hail a cab would you –

PARKER: Yes sir.

DORIAN: I must change.

*PARKER exits.*

BASIL: *(Calling after DORIAN.)* Don't forget!

DORIAN: *(Exiting.)* I won't!

BASIL: *(To LORD HENRY.)* You do remember what I asked you this morning Harry –

LORD HENRY: What was that?

BASIL: I trust you.

LORD HENRY: Dear Basil…if only I could trust myself!

*Laughter and a round of applause, as if that was the curtain line of the act.*

*The unhappy, wounded is BASIL left looking at his picture for consolation.*

*Music – the entr'acte at the theatre, as –*

*The ladies of the CHORUS sweep on stage, in their gowns – diamonds and trains, fluttering programmes and ostrich fans.*

BASIL: *(Calling the FOOTMEN to remove the painting.)* Thank you.

*The CHORUS watch, suspended. The black canvas is carried across the stage.*

*(Calling to start the next scene.)* Thank you!

## SCENE TWO
## THE FOYER OF A WEST END THEATRE. A MONTH LATER

*A trio of Society Ladies install themselves centre stage and scan the passing trade. Two West End Stage-door Jonnies watch them*

LADY RUXTON: Dorian *who?*

LADY NARBORUGH: His mother was a Devereaux apparently. Lady *Margaret* Devereaux?

MRS. ERLYNNE: Goodness what an ugly story that was. And she could have married anybody she chose. Good-looking?

LADY NARBOROUGH: Very. And well-off of course. Now.

LADY RUXTON: Then I do hope he will fall into the proper hands.

MRS ERLYNNE: Young people nowadays imagine money is everything.

LADY RUXTON: Yes and when they grow older, they know it. Do you care for the play?

LADY NARBOROUGH: No. Dreadfully superficial, so far. Do you?

LADY RUXTON: No.

LADY NARBOROUGH: What martyrs we are, Olivia.

MRS ERLYNNE: And how well it becomes us.

LADY CARLISLE: *(Steaming on.)* Lady Victoria!

*LADY VICTORIA WOTTON is very grand, and has straw-coloured hair. Having to make conversation with a do-gooder causes her almost physical pain.*

LADY WOTTON: Lady Carlisle. And how is Whitechapel?

LADY CARLISLE: Oh, so unhappy – it is really most distressing.

LADY WOTTON: I can sympathise with everything except suffering – there is something so morbid in this modern sympathy with pain. The less said about life sores, the better.

LADY CARLISLE: Still, the East End is a very important problem.

LADY WOTTON: Quite so. It is the problem of slavery, –

*An electric bell (rung by FRANCIS) sounds for the end of the interval – people start to return to their seats.*

– and we try to solve it by amusing the slaves.

LADY CARLISLE: But what change do you propose?

LADY WOTTON: I don't desire to change anything in England except the weather.

LADY CARLISLE: But we have such grave responsibilities, –

LORD HENRY: Terribly grave, Lady Agatha.

*LORD HENRY and DORIAN are immaculate in conspicuously matching white waistcoats and gloves and buttonholes; Master and Pupil. They have been inseparable for the past month.*

LADY CARLISLE: Ah! Lord Henry – and Mr Gray. Now, I thought Schumann's *Forest Scenes* next week, Mr. Gray – so leafy, and yet respectable. Ah! –

*She has spotted her next victim;*

– Lady Barford. Do excuse me – *(Sternly; evidently LADY BARFORD is trying to escape…)* Lady Barford!!

*Exits.*

LORD HENRY: *(To his wife.)* Victoria, may I present Mr –

LADY WOTTON: Dorian Gray. Yes, I know.

DORIAN: Lady Wotton.

LADY WOTTON: From your photographs, Mr Gray. I think my husband has collected seventeen of them in the past month. Or is it eighteen, Harry?

LORD HENRY: Repetition converts romance into an art. Or so I'm told.

LADY WOTTON: And I saw you together at the opera the other night. Dear *Lohengrin* – so loud one can talk the whole time without other people hearing what one says. That is a great advantage, don't you think, Mr Gray?

DORIAN: *(Giving a passable imitation of LORD HENRY.)* I am afraid I don't Lady Henry; I never talk during music – at least, during good music. If one hears bad music, it is one's duty to drown it in conversation.

*Bell!*

LADY WOTTON: *(With savage condescension.)* Ah; that is one of Harry's views. I always hear Harry's views from his friends. *(Moving to leave.)* Do come to one of my parties, Mr Gray – I can't afford orchids, but I spare no expense in strangers and foreigners. Harry, you are dining out, I suppose. So am I. Perhaps I shall see you at Lady Thornbury's.

LORD HENRY: Perhaps.

LADY WOTTON: *(To DORIAN as she goes.)* Such a pleasure.

*She leaves. LORD HENRY stares after her.*

LORD HENRY: Dorian –

*Bell! LADY CARLISLE makes a last minute grab as she hurries to get back to her seat in time –*

LADY CARLISLE: Lord Henry – *might* you be disengaged Tuesday?

LORD HENRY: For you I would throw over anybody, Lady Carlisle.

*LADY CARLISLE gurgles with delight and smacks LORD HENRY with her fan. As she looks at the gorgeous DORIAN, in what she fondly imagines is a girlish whisper;*

LADY CARLISLE: Oh Lord Henry, I wish you would tell me how to become young again.

LORD HENRY: Can you remember any great error that you committed in your early days, Lady Carlisle?

LADY CARLISLE: A great many, I fear.

LORD HENRY: Then commit them over again. The only things we never regret in life are our mistakes.

LADY CARLISLE: Oh what a dreadful theory. I must put it into practice at once.

*Bell! She exits with a final shriek.*

LORD HENRY: *(Still thinking of his wife.)* Never marry a woman with straw-coloured hair, Dorian.

DORIAN: Why?

LORD HENRY: Because they are so sentimental. In fact, never marry at all. Men marry because they are tired; women marry because they are curious. Both are disappointed.

DORIAN: O, I don't think I am likely to ever marry. Harry.

*This is the first time DORIAN has dared to call him HARRY.*

LORD HENRY: Good boy.

*Long Final Bell!! The foyer is now empty – except for one of the JOHNNIES, who is looking offstage as if after a woman, loitering.*

LORD HENRY: Cigarette?

*LORD HENRY offers DORIAN a cigarette. They clearly have no intention whatever of going in to the play.*

*Referring to his gold cigarette case;*

Do keep it.

*DORIAN accepts the gift with a gesture that exactly mimics one of LORD HENRY's; there is applause and a brief flourish from a pit orchestra as the curtain rises on Act Two of the unseen play. The JOHNNY turns and looks, as –*

### SCENE THREE
### DORIAN'S HOUSE

*Jump cut; DORIAN is alone, and deep in thought.*

*Still holding the unlit cigarette, he picks up his hand mirror, and inspects his face.*

*As he stares at himself, LORD HENRY, in the shadows, stares at him…*

DORIAN: When did the man from Albemarle Street say the picture was going to arrive Victor?

VICTOR: *(The JOHNNY, becoming a new character. French accent.)* **In one month, monsieur.**

DORIAN: I shall be jealous – it will be a whole month younger than myself.

VICTOR: **Yes m'sieur.** *(Awaiting instructions – DORIAN is busy gazing in his mirror.)* **M'sieur?**

DORIAN: Oh – yes. I'm dining at Kettner's with Lord Henry. He says the lampshades are the most becoming in London. And then we'll be at White's I imagine.

*At the mention of Kettner's, and at FRANCIS' instruction, the men begin to set up a dining table around DORIAN.*

VICTOR: **Yes m'sieur.**

DORIAN: No need to stay up.

VICTOR: **Non m'sieur.**

*MRS LEAF finally moves from her chair; as the WAITERS bustle with chairs, she moves to transform herself into MRS. VANE.*

FRANCIS: *(As a MAITRE d' offers DORIAN a light for his cigarette.)* **Sir?**

DORIAN: What? Oh thank you.

FRANCIS: **Thank *you*.**

*The sounds of a restaurant; we jump-cut into the next scene –*

SCENE FOUR
AFTER DINNER AT KETTNER'S AND SIMULTANEOUSLY
BACKSTAGE IN POPLAR. ANOTHER MONTH LATER

*DORIAN has changed considerably from the gauche creature we first met – he is now a very highly polished reflection of his tutor.*

DORIAN: Oh, I don't think I am likely to *marry* her, Harry. I am too much in love for that.

LORD HENRY: My dear boy –

DORIAN: Yes I know – one of yours. Well, I'm putting it into practice – as I do everything you say. *(To a passing WAITER.)* Deux fine-champagnes, merci.

WAITER: Sir.

LORD HENRY: And who are you in love with?

DORIAN: An actress.

LORD HENRY: That's a rather commonplace *debut.*

DORIAN: You wouldn't say so if you saw her, Harry.

LORD HENRY: Who is she?

DORIAN: Her name is Sybil Vane.

LORD HENRY: Never heard of her.

DORIAN: No one has. But they will, one day. Harry, she's a genius.

LORD HENRY: My dear Dorian no woman is a genius –

DORIAN: Harry how can you –

LORD HENRY: It is quite true. And I ought to know… There are only two kinds of women; the plain, and the coloured. The plain women are very useful – if you want to gain a reputation for respectability you have merely to take them down to supper; the other women meanwhile are very charming. They commit one mistake, however; they paint in order to try and look young. Our grandmothers were wiser; they painted in order to try and talk brilliantly. *Rouge* and *esprit* used to go together. Nowadays of course so long as a woman can look ten years younger than her own daughter she is perfectly satisfied, and as for conversation, there are only five women in London worth talking to, and two of them can't be admitted into decent society. *(Satisfied that his rebellious pupil has been put back in his place, he returns to the point; bluntly.)* How long have you known her?

DORIAN: About three weeks.

LORD HENRY: And where did you "come across" her?

DORIAN: You mustn't be unsympathetic, Harry – it would never have happened if I hadn't met you.

LORD HENRY: Really?

DORIAN: You've taught me curiosity – curiosity about other people and the strange and sordid lives they sometimes lead. What else could possibly have lead me to find myself at half-past eight one Wednesday night outside an absurd little theatre in a grimy East End backstreet – and to pay an entire guinea for a box.

*Footlights have started to glow again; a tired stage-hand – DANNY – sweeps a dim stage. From now on we see the restaurant and the theatre simultaneously. Gradually two more STAGEHANDS begin to fly in ropes and move scenery.*

DANNY: Miss Vane!

DORIAN: It was horrid, a sort of tawdry, third-rate wedding cake inside – but if I hadn't gone in, I should have missed the greatest romance of my life.

DANNY: Half an hour, Miss Vane!

LORD HENRY: The *first* romance of your life, you should say.

DORIAN: Do you really think me that shallow?

LORD HENRY: My dear boy it is people who only love once who are shallow. What they call fidelity, I call lack of imagination. What was the play?

DORIAN: Oh, it was good enough even for you Harry – *Romeo and Juliet.* And when she came on – *(The love-struck young man showing through the aesthete;)* Oh Harry, she's seventeen.

*A STAGE-HAND whistles to the flyman. SYBIL VANE runs on, barefooted, and starts touching up her make-up in a piece of mirror. A breathless natural beauty – and young.*

LORD HENRY: Is she…

DORIAN: Why did you never tell me the only thing worth loving is an actress?

LORD HENRY: Because I have loved so many of them.

DORIAN: Yes – horrid people with dyed hair and painted faces.

*MRS VANE emerges from the backstage shadows and knocks back a brandy. A shabby, filthy old wrapper over a gown. She watches SYBIL like a hawk.*

LORD HENRY: Don't run down dyed hair and painted faces, Dorian. There is an extraordinary charm in them, sometimes. And tell me – reach me the matches would you, like a good boy – tell me; is she your mistress already?

DORIAN: *(Furious – pushing back his chair.)* Harry how dare you. *(Controlling himself.)* Sybil Vane is sacred.

*The waiter stares.*

*SYBIL inspects her body with the mirror; proud of what she sees.*

LORD HENRY: It is only the sacred things that are worth touching, Dorian. Do sit down. But you do know her, I take it?

DORIAN: Of course I know her.

LORD HENRY: And when did you first speak to her?

DORIAN: Not until the third night. I go every single night, now –

*MRS VANE enters the room.*

DANNY: *(With a bouquet of red roses.)* Flowers for Miss Vane. Again!

DORIAN: I couldn't be happy, if I didn't see her every night.

SYBIL: Thanks Danny.

LORD HENRY: Of course you couldn't.

SYBIL: No card?

DANNY: What d'you think?

MRS. VANE: *(Coming forward to help SYBIL get into costume, and shooing DANNY out.)* Yes thank you dear.

DORIAN: Harry say something! She's the only thing I care about.

SYBIL: *(Checking her lines through under her breath.)*
Thou knowest the mask of night is on my face…the mask…of night…

LORD HENRY: What do you propose to do?

DORIAN: Do?

LORD HENRY: Have you mentioned the word *marriage*?

MRS. VANE: *(Simultaneously with LORD HENRY.)* Has he mentioned the word marriage?

SYBIL: Oh Mother!! I'm *happy* – and you should be too.

DORIAN: Not yet.

*He thinks, as;*

MRS VANE: I am only happy, Sybil, when I see you act. You must not think of anything but your acting. Mr. Isaacs here has been very good to us, and we owe him money. Fifty pounds to pay your brother's passage to the colonies… Fifty pounds is a very large sum.

SYBIL: Mr Isaacs is not a gentleman. And we don't need him any more.

MRS VANE: You listen to me my girl…

DORIAN: *(Suddenly standing up and calling for the bill.)* Garcon!!

MRS VANE: *(Spinning her round and shaking her.)* Sybil!!

*JAMES VANE enters the dressing room with a kitbag. The women postpone their confrontation.*

JAMES: Mother…

DORIAN: I want you and Basil to come with me and see her act, and then you can tell me what to do. I warn you, she'll make you as mad as she has made me –

LORD HENRY: I doubt that will be possible. When?

DORIAN: Tomorrow!

*DORIAN prepares to leave, is brought his hat and cape by the Maitre d' (FRANCIS), leaves money carelessly on the table, slips on his perfect white gloves…*

MRS VANE: *(Collecting herself.)* Good evening James.

*She seems oddly cowed by her son. She dresses SYBIL.*

LORD HENRY: Very well. Shall you see Basil, or shall I write to him?

DORIAN: Perhaps you'd better write. It's rather horrid of me but I prefer not to see Basil alone just now. He's become a bit of a Philistine – he always gives me good advice.

LORD HENRY: People are always fond of giving away what they most need themselves. It is what I call the depths of generosity.

*DORIAN laughs.*

DORIAN: He does rather lack romance.

HENRY: Really. Has he ever talked to you about that?

DORIAN: *(Not picking up the hint at all.)* Never. He sent me my portrait, by the way. In the most wonderful frame – designed by himself. I must go – the curtain rises at seven, and Juliet is waiting for me. I shall find her by moonlight, in an orchard in Verona.

*LORD HENRY watches DORIAN dash away, leaves a large tip for the handsome waiter.*

LORD HENRY: I'm sure you shall…

*He finishes his cigarette and looks after DORIAN.*

*The STAGE HANDS who have been crossing the stage with ladders and ropes have flown in what looks like a canvas flat for* Romeo and Juliet, *covered in a burlap cloth. The hum of the gathering audience out in the auditorium is audible; backstage, the pace quickens.*

DANNY: *(Onstage, to the crew.)* Five minutes everybody!!

MRS VANE: Well I must say the whole thing is most inconvenient, what with your brother here setting sail in the morning and me having so much to think of. You could have shown more consideration Sybil, really you might. However, if the young gentleman is rich –

DANNY: *(Shouting in a backstage corridor.)* Five minutes please!!

JAMES: *(Looking at the roses.)* He's coming again tonight then? Your *gentleman*?

MRS VANE: In the profession, James, a young lady of talent must become accustomed to receiving a great deal of gratifying attention. I myself used to receive bouquets at one time. And there is no doubt that the young man in question is a gentleman. He is always most polite to me –

JAMES: You don't know his name though.

SYBIL: Jim, not the night before you leave, please –

MRS VANE: No she doesn't, which I think is most romantic of him. He is probably a member of the aristocracy.

JAMES: If I come back from Australia one day and find he has done my sister any wrong, I shall kill him.

*DANNY knocks and pokes his head round the dressing room door.*

JAMES: *(Shouting.)* I said, I shall kill him.

SYBIL: Stop it Jim!!

DANNY: Er, Overture and Beginners… Mrs. Vane ma'am? Scene One?

MRS VANE: Certainly. Very effectively put, James, and I am sure we shall all laugh about it some day, but we are not giving *The Sailor's Revenge*, tonight.

*She removes her wrapper, and sweeps out in character as Lady Capulet.*

JAMES: *(Tenderly.)* Sis?

SYBIL: I do know his name.

JAMES: What is it then?

SYBIL: *(Smiling to herself as she lies.)* Prince Charming.

*The audience applauds as the curtain rises on* Romeo and Juliet…

Oh Jim – if you only saw his face.

I shall love him always.

Always.

DANNY: Miss Vane! Miss Vane! You're on!

*SYBIL runs to the stage.*

*The performance begins; a rally from the pit-band and a round from the audience as the curtain goes up.*

*JAMES VANE shoulders his bag, and leaves.*

## SCENE FIVE
## LONDON, THAT NIGHT

*LORD HENRY, on his way home from Kettner's, pauses to talk to the audience.*

LORD HENRY: **Human life…is there anything else worth investigating? So rarely do we understand ourselves – and experience is of no value; it is merely the name we give to our mistakes. So, the boy was in love – prematurely; but sometimes, to be premature is to be perfect. One can never, I think, pay too high a price for any sensation…but I did wonder how it was all going to end. When I got home –**

A TELEGRAPH DELIVERY BOY: **…telegram for you my Lord.**

LORD HENRY: **…there was a telegram waiting for me.**
*(To the TELEGRAPH BOY:)* **No.**

> **"Engaged to be married to Sybil Vane."**

## SCENE SIX
### CHEZ LORD HENRY, CURZON STREET,
### AND ONSTAGE IN POPLAR. THE NEXT NIGHT

*Throughout this scene, LORD HENRY is impatiently changing his gloves and scarf and putting on his opera cape – adjusting his make-up, checking his watch – eager to head out to the theatre. His agitation (a rare occurrence) betrays his disquiet – his annoyance – with the fact that DORIAN may have found a replacement for LORD HENRY in his affections…and also his impatience with BASIL's moralising. FRANCIS, as ever implacably ushering the tragedy forward on its appointed course, watches, and prompts his staff to assist if required.*

*BASIL has just received the news.*

BASIL: I don't believe it!

LORD HENRY: It is perfectly true.

BASIL: Dorian is far too sensible.

LORD HENRY: Dorian is far too wise not to do foolish things now and then, my dear Basil.

BASIL: Marriage is hardly a thing one can do now and then, Harry.

LORD HENRY: I didn't say he was married. I said he was engaged to be married. There is a great difference. I have a distinct remembrance of being married, but I have no recollection at all of being engaged.

BASIL: I just hope the girl is good.

LORD HENRY: Oh she is better than good – she is beautiful.

BASIL: Are you ever serious, Harry?

LORD HENRY: Rarely. But I should be miserable if I thought I should ever be more serious than I am at the present moment.

BASIL: So you approve?

LORD HENRY: I never approve or disapprove of anything nowadays, Basil. We are not sent into this world to air our moral prejudices. Dorian Gray falls in love with a beautiful girl who acts Juliet, and proposes to marry her. Why not? If he wedded Messalina he would be none the less interesting. I hope he will make this girl his wife, adore her for six months, and then become fascinated by someone else… It will be wonderful to watch.

BASIL: You don't mean a single word of that. You know you don't.

LORD HENRY: *(Almost snapping.)* You do know, Basil, that the reason we all think so well of others is that we are afraid for ourselves? The basis of optimism is sheer terror… Of course, there are other and more interesting bonds between men and women than marriage. I shall certainly encourage them. They have the charm of being fashionable.

BASIL: I hope one touch of this girl's hand will make him forget you. You, and all your poisonous theories.

LORD HENRY: And those are? *(Calling his manservant.)* Lane!

BASIL: Your theories about life, about love, about pleasure. Your theories about everything, in fact.

LORD HENRY: Pleasure is the only thing worth having a theory about Basil. When we are happy, we are always good, but when we are good we are not always happy.

BASIL: What do you mean by good? I asked you what you meant by good, Harry?

LORD HENRY: *(Stopping for the only moment in the scene; exasperated at being obliged to declare his credo – but swiftly lapsing back into phrase-making.)* To be good is to be in harmony with one's self. Believe me, Basil, no civilised man ever regrets a pleasure, just as no uncivilised man ever knows what a pleasure is. Lane!!!

LANE: **Yes Sir?**

*LORD HENRY angrily collects his hat and cane. He puts on his gloves.*

LORD HENRY: The cab.

LANE: **Yes Sir.**

BASIL: But surely if one lives entirely for oneself, one pays a terrible price.

LORD HENRY: Yes, we are overcharged for everything nowadays.

We should go – who knows, this wonderful girl of Dorian's may even provide us with the thrill of some new emotion.

I do love acting. It is so much more real than life.

*Despite himself, BASIL laughs.*

*In the theatre, the sound of slow-handclaps, boos, hisses from a disgruntled theatre audience. Cries of "Off, Off."*

BASIL: Harry, you are dreadful. I don't know why I like you so much.

LORD HENRY: Because I represent to you all the sins you have never had the courage to commit.

BASIL: Is that quite true?

LORD HENRY: Nothing is ever *quite* true, Basil.

*They leave for the theatre; the boos and catcalls reach a crescendo, as…*

## SCENE SEVEN
### THE CURTAIN CALL IN IN POPLAR, LATER THAT NIGHT

*Silhouetted against footlights, SYBIL (almost getting the giggles), defiantly – extravagantly – takes her farewell bow in a storm of abuse…*

*She runs backstage.*

## SCENE EIGHT
### BACKSTAGE IN POPLAR.  LATER THAT NIGHT

*SYBIL starts cold-creaming her face, laughing to herself.*

*DORIAN watches her. He is in full "Prince Charming" evening dress. He says nothing, and his face dead and white.*

*SYBIL catches sight of him in her mirror – she gasps in fright –*

SYBIL: Oh! Dorian…

> *She goes back to cleaning her face.*

> You do understand, don't you?

DORIAN: *(In a voice as cold and hard as marble.)* Understand what?

SYBIL: Why I was so bad tonight. Why I shall never act again. Before I knew you, I thought it was all true. "Thou knowest the mask of night is on my face, else would a maiden blush bepaint my cheek" *(She laughs.)*…but when you came, you taught me what reality really is. You taught me what love really is. Now I've got you, I don't need anything else. No more scenery, no more painted moonlight… Take me away. Take me away with you. My Prince Charming…

DORIAN: I will never see you again. I will never think of you. I will never even mention your name.

SYBIL: *(Laughing.)* What do you mean?

DORIAN: I would have made you famous – splendid, magnificent. What are you now? A third-rate actress with a pretty face.

SYBIL: Dorian…

DORIAN: My friends were bored!!!!! *I* was bored.

SYBIL: You are acting.

DORIAN: Acting! I leave that to you. You do it so well. Don't touch me!!

SYBIL: But I was thinking of *you*... I was thinking of you, all the time – that's why I was so bad...I'm sorry I didn't act well, and I will try. I promise I will. It's all just been so sudden...

*DORIAN goes to leave.*

If you leave me, my brother'll kill you – !! No, no he wouldn't. He didn't mean that. I will work so hard, you'll see. Kiss me. Come on, kiss me. Don't leave me. Don't leave me...don't leave me...

*DORIAN leaves the room. SYBIL collapses.*

*With the image of SYBIL sobbing and dying behind him, lit by the lurid glare of dying footlights, DORIAN is like a figure from a Victorian melodrama. His voice is hard and elegant.*

DORIAN: **There is always something ridiculous about the emotions of people whom one has ceased to love. Don't you find?**

*SYBIL turns – and tears at the cloth covering the piece of scenery. The cloth falls, revealing the golden-framed picture. Whatever it is she sees in it, it makes her scream.*

SYBIL: Ah!!

*The CHORUS begin to press onstage.*

## SCENE NINE
## GROSVENOR SQUARE. DAWN

*As he describes his walk home, DORIAN is supremely calm. He smokes – taking his cigarette, we notice, from LORD HENRY's gold cigarette-case – and for the first time we see not a charming young beauty, but a perfectly dressed psychopath in a state of dissociated shock. As he speaks, MRS. LEAF stares accusingly at DORIAN; SYBIL's sobbing turns into a weird choking – and then she lies quiet and still.*

DORIAN: **Where I went, I hardly knew. I remember walking through a labyrinth of dimly-lit streets, across black, grassless squares... Women with hoarse voices and harsh laughter called out after me;**

MRS. LEAF: *(In MRS VANE's voice.)* **Prince Charming...**

DORIAN:

                              **drunkards reeled by, cursing.**

**A man with curious eyes dogged my footsteps.**

**It was dawn before I found myself in Piccadilly Circus. There was something in the dawn's loveliness that seemed to me inexpressibly pathetic; I thought of all the days that break in beauty, and set in storm. There were some carters, on their way to Covent Garden, and I wondered what they thought of me; whether they knew anything of this city's splendour and its shame...its fierce, fiery-coloured joys; its horrible hunger. What a strange London they see...a city free from the smoke of night and the sin of day; a pallid, ghost-like city. I envied them everything they did not know.**

*The full CHORUS are now visible onstage. They are clearly waiting for something to happen to DORIAN... Their stares suggest that they know something he doesn't...*

*DORIAN arrives home.*

*It is now dawn.*

*DORIAN loosens his tie, and looks at himself in a handheld mirror.*

*DEAD SYBIL stands up and joins the CHORUS.*

*In the mirror, DORIAN sees the picture – just as SYBIL saw him…*

*A slight lurch of shock; the CHORUS of figures echoes his quiet gasp…*

*Looking in the mirror, DORIAN compares his face with the face in the picture.*

*Insinuating voices begin to whisper in his head…;*

**CHORUS; "A LITTLE CHANGED"**

**FEMALE CHORUS:** *How curious. The face…*

**LADY NARBOROUGH'S VOICE:** The face seemed to be a little changed. The expression looked…different.

**LADY WOTTON'S VOICE:** One might have said there was a touch of cruelty about the mouth –

**LADY RUXTON'S VOICE:** As if he had done some…dreadful thing.

**BASIL:** *What did that mean?*

**CHORUS:** *What did that mean?*

**DEAD SYBIL:** *"What do you mean?"*

**MRS VANE'S VOICE:** …Prince Charming.

*He checks again in the mirror. He scrutinises the picture.*

DORIAN: Impossible.

**CHORUS:** *Impossible, surely…*

*Surely;*

*Surely his mad wish had not been fulfilled?*

*You remember;*

*"If only it were the other way. If only it were I who was to be always young, and the picture that was to grow old…"*

*His mad wish that his beauty might be kept untarnished –*

*That what he dreamed, it would realise…*

*But that would be impossible.*

> *Impossible, that for every sin he now committed, a stain would wreck and fleck the surface of the picture...*
>
> *Impossible – and horrible...*
>
> *Horrible.*

**LADY WOTTON: Cruelty? Well, *had* he been cruel?**

DORIAN: *(Talking to the voices, defending himself.)* That was her fault, not mine.

**FRANCIS: The girl *had* been shallow and unworthy, but surely...**

**LADY WOTTON: Surely a painted canvas could not alter... Surely...**

DORIAN: Victor!

*VICTOR steps into character; the Chorus wait.*

VICTOR: Monsieur?

*DORIAN wants to ask him to look at the picture with him, to see if what he fears has happened has indeed happened – but he daren't.*

DORIAN: Victor, could you...

VICTOR: Monsieur? *(Noticing something is wrong.)* You are cold, M'sieur?

DORIAN: I don't think so. Thank you. I just wondered... Coffee, this morning, please.

*(As VICTOR goes.)* And the key to the dining room.

VICTOR: Monsieur?

DORIAN: You do have it.

VICTOR: Of course M'sieur –

*VICTOR collects the keys from MRS LEAF and gives them to DORIAN.*

DORIAN: Thank you. And I'm not at home to anyone this morning.

VICTOR: M'sieur.

*Unable to stand the pressure of not knowing if the picture has really changed on not, DORIAN locks the door.*

*DORIAN hesitates –*

**MRS LEAF:** *Do it.*

*Braces himself – and turns and looks at the picture again.*

*The voices return…;*

**CHORUS; "A LITTLE CHANGE"** (2)

*Ah!*

*It was true;*

*Quite true.*

*(Nothing is* quite *true – )*

*It had altered.*

*The gold hair, the blue eyes, the red lips – they were all there –*

*And beautiful, still –*

*Beautiful – bright, clear, gleaming –*

*But altered. Warped –*

*Marred –*

*Changed.*

*Cruel.*

*Viciously cruel…*

*Why had he been made like that?*

*How terrible.*

*How absurd.*

*Monstrous, even to think of.*

*But…*

*The voices cleverly – poisonously – prompt his useless change of heart.*

*But surely it was not too late. He could change.*

*He could – he* would *resist temptation –*

*not see Lord Henry any more –*

*not listen to a single poisonous word – and...;*

*he'd write a letter.*

*The CHORUS repeat their prompt;*

*He'd write a letter.*

*DORIAN grabs a pen and paper and prepares to scribble a letter –*

*– He'd go back to Sybil; make amends – try to love her, and...*

MRS LEAF AS MRS. VANE: **Marry her.**

DEAD SYBIL: *(Vindictively.)* ***Marry her!***

THE VOICES: ***Marry her... Yes, that was it.***

DORIAN: My darling...

*As he scribbles furiously;*

MALE CHORUS: *(Parodying DORIAN's outpouring in his letter – rushed, breathy, adolescent);*

***"My darling during these last few terrible hours I have lived centuries of pain. If I have wounded you, it was because my soul was shaped for suffering..."***

FEMALE CHORUS: *(Implacably, as they leave.)* **Beautiful, of course, but-**

MALE CHORUS: ***"Forgive me. I have been selfish and cruel – "***

FEMALE CHORUS: **Warped.**

MALE CHORUS: ***" – spoken wild words of sorrow and wilder words of pain"***

FEMALE CHORUS: **Corrupted.**

MALE CHORUS: ***"The scarlet threads of my life have tangled. Forgive me,***

> ***my darling, you whose lips were made for the madness of kisses; Forgive me –***

> ***forgive me –***

> ***forgive me..."***

*The LADIES retreat as the MEN mock DORIAN's letter.*

**DEAD SYBIL:** *(Vengefully, as she leaves – the last to leave.)*
**By the time he'd finished it, he felt sure he'd been forgiven already…**

*There is a sudden knocking on the locked door.*

*DORIAN starts up in guilt, swiftly finishes the letter and conceals it,.*

*He goes to open the door. FRANCIS intercepts and reminds him of the picture.*

FRANCIS: The picture.

*He hurriedly throws something over it and goes the door.*

LORD HENRY: *(Outside the room.)* Dorian, you must let me in.

My dear boy, I must see you. I cannot bear you shutting yourself up like this. Dorian!

*DORIAN unlocks the door.*

*The MALE CHORUS are still onstage, watching throughout.*

## SCENE TEN
## THE END OF THAT MORNING

*The scene is witnessed by the MALE CHORUS – and of course MRS LEAF.*

*LORD HENRY is carrying a copy of* The Standard.

LORD HENRY: My dear boy, I am so sorry – but it was not your fault.

DORIAN: Do you mean Sybil?

LORD HENRY: Of course. Tell me, did you make a scene with her, after the play was over?

DORIAN: A perfectly brutal one. But it's alright – it has taught me to know myself better.

LORD HENRY: I am so glad you take it in that way. I was afraid I'd find you plunged in remorse and tearing that remarkable hair of yours.

DORIAN: I'm going to marry her.

LORD HENRY: Marry her? But my dear boy –

DORIAN: Please don't say something dreadful about marriage Harry; Sybil Vane is going to be my wife.

LORD HENRY: You didn't get my letter then?

DORIAN: Your letter?

*LORD HENRY takes hold of DORIAN's hands.*

LORD HENRY: I sent it round this morning. Dorian – don't be frightened – my letter was to tell you that Sybil Vane is dead.

DORIAN: It isn't true.

LORD HENRY: It is quite true Dorian, it's in all the morning papers.

It seems she swallowed some dreadful thing they use in theatres, with prussic acid or white lead in it. It is very tragic of course, but you must not get mixed up in it – one should never make one's *debut* with a scandal, at least not in London. People are so prejudiced – and I see from *The*

43

*Standard* that she was actually younger than seventeen. I don't suppose anyone knew your name at the theatre?

DORIAN: I have murdered her. Murdered her as surely as if I had cut her throat. What shall I do?

*LORD HENRY pauses, then launches his counter-attack.*

LORD HENRY: My dear Dorian, it often happens that the tragedies of life occur in an inartistic manner; they hurt us by their absurd want of meaning – their entire lack of style. But in the present case, what is it that has happened? Someone has killed themselves for love of you. I assure you, Dorian, not one of the women I have known would have done for me what Sybil Vane has done for you. I am glad to be living in a century where such wonders happen. It makes one almost believe in the reality of the things we all play with. In Romance. Passion.

In Love.

*DORIAN turns to look at the (covered) portrait.*

DORIAN: I had such good intentions.

LORD HENRY: Good intentions are a useless attempt to interfere with scientific laws. Their origin is pure vanity and their result absolutely nil. They are cheques drawn on a bank where a weak man has no account, and that is all that can be said for them.

*(Changing tack; seductively.)* I have never seen you really and absolutely angry, Dorian, but I can fancy how delightful you looked. I'm sure you were splendid. Don't waste your tears on Sybil Vane. She has played her last part. It was all simply a scene from some strange, tragic play.

*A beat.*

DORIAN: Harry, you explain me to myself.

*DORIAN turns round; shockingly, he is radiant; transformed. He takes out a cigarette from his golden cigarette case.*

But let's not talk of it again. I wonder if life has still in store for me any experience this marvellous.

LORD HENRY: Good boy. Life has everything in store for you. With your looks, there is nothing that you will not be able to do.

*LORD HENRY light's DORIAN's cigarette.*

DORIAN: Nothing? But suppose I become old, and haggard, and wrinkled – what then?

LORD HENRY: Ah, then…then, my dear Dorian, you will have to fight for your victories. Meanwhile, since we live in an age that reads too much to be wise, and thinks too much to be beautiful, we cannot spare you. We'd better drive down to the club to eat – we're rather late as it is.

DORIAN: I think I shall join you at the Opera. What number is your sister's box?

LORD HENRY: Twenty-seven, I believe. Grand Tier. Are you sure you won't dine?

DORIAN: I don't feel up to it…thanks.

*A warm and intimate stare from LORD HENRY; a perfect lie of a smile from DORIAN.*

LORD HENRY: We'll see you before nine-thirty, I hope. Patti is singing, remember.

*LORD HENRY leaves.*

*DORIAN marches across the room to the picture and pulls away the cover.*

*He inhales deeply from his cigarette, and says to the audience;*

DORIAN: **Nothing. Nothing I cannot do.**

**Eternal… Youth.**

**Thank you.**

**Thank you!**

## SCENE ELEVEN
## DORIAN GOES TO THE OPERA

*Patti sings Bellini's "La Sonnambula". The picture glows with golden promise.*

**CHORUS; "THE PROMISE"**

**FRANCIS:**   ***Eternal Youth…***

   ***Infinite passion;***

   ***Pleasures subtle and secret.***


   ***Wild joys, and wilder sins…and hour by hour,
   week by week, the portrait –***

   ***– not him, but his portrait –***

   ***was to bear the burden of his
shame. That was all.***

   ***That, was all.***

*As the sound of the opera swells orgasmically, DORIAN gazes at his picture as if it were the most beautiful and gratifying mirror in the world.*

*He drinks a glass of champagne. All is peace and beauty.*

*The Footmen heave on a rope, and a great embroidered velvet pall descends and covers the picture – one expressive of DORIAN's new pride and pleasure in the portrait. But….*

*But it must be kept covered from now on.*

*MRS LEAF watches, as ever. The CHORUS OF MEN begin to leave, as –*

*BASIL bursts into DORIAN's room. The music is suddenly cut off by the sound of the needle being ripped across a phonograph –*

## SCENE TWELVE
## THE NEXT MORNING

*BASIL has charged into DORIAN's room.*

BASIL: You went to the Opera!?!

FRANCIS: **Wild joys – and wilder sins...**

BASIL: You went to the Opera, while Sybil Vane was lying dead in some sordid lodging on the Euston Road!?!

DORIAN: Yes. Patti sang divinely. What's past is past, Basil.

BASIL: You call yesterday the past?

DORIAN: Only shallow people require years to get rid of an emotion.

BASIL: Something has changed you. You look exactly the same wonderful boy who used to come down to my studio to sit for his picture – but now you talk as if you had no heart. No pity. I blame Harry. If –

DORIAN: *(Cutting him off.)* Basil, what do you want?

BASIL: The Dorian Gray I used to paint.

DORIAN: In which case I'm afraid you have come too late. Yesterday, I suffered immensely. But I cannot repeat an emotion. Do sit down.

*BASIL has noticed the picture.*

BASIL: Why's it covered up?

DORIAN: What?

BASIL: The picture.

*A beat.*

DORIAN: The light was too strong.

BASIL: Surely not. That's an admirable place for it –

DORIAN: You mustn't look at it –

BASIL: Why on earth not, it's my own work. Did I tell you I plan to exhibit it in Paris this autumn? –

DORIAN: If you touch that I will never speak to you again. I am quite serious, Basil. Exhibit it!

BASIL: Dorian –

DORIAN: Don't speak!

BASIL: Of course I won't look at it if you don't want me to. I'm sorry.

*DORIAN decides how he is going to silence BASIL. There is now a new note of calculation in his voice.*

DORIAN: Basil, Harry tells me you once told him you would never exhibit this picture. Why was that?

*A silence.*

BASIL: If I told you, you might like me even less than you do.

DORIAN: Then it seems we each of us have a secret. Let me know yours, and I might tell you mine.

*BASIL turns ashen, then steadies himself and makes a decision.*

BASIL: Very well. Do you mind if I have a drink?

DORIAN: Not at all.

BASIL: Have you ever noticed something curious about the picture – something that probably didn't strike you at first, but then slowly revealed itself?

*A beat. DORIAN works hard to conceal a sudden fear.*

DORIAN: No.

BASIL: I see you did. Now it is your turn not to speak.

Dorian, you are my ideal. From the first moment I saw you, I quite admit it, I worshipped you – worshipped you with far more romance of feeling than a man usually gives or should ever give to a friend. Somehow, I have never loved a woman. I suppose I never had the time… I adored you. Madly. Extravagantly. Absurdly. I was jealous of everyone to whom you spoke. I was only happy when I was with you. Of course, I never let you know any of this, it would have been impossible – you wouldn't have understood it. I hardly understood it myself. But when I was painting…when I was painting, every flake and film of colour revealed my secret. Every line was filled with love. Every touch of scarlet; every stroke of gold in your marvellous hair. I *worshipped* you.

*BASIL's declaration of his love has brought him to the edge of tears.*

You saw it, didn't you?

DORIAN: Something like that.

BASIL: Can I look at it now?

DORIAN: I'm afraid not, Basil.

BASIL: Do you have any idea what it has cost a man like me to tell you what I have just told you?

DORIAN: What, that you once liked me too much? That isn't even a compliment.

BASIL: It wasn't intended as a compliment. It was a confession.

DORIAN: A very disappointing one.

But I'm sure we can remain friends. Good bye, Basil.

*BASIL leaves.*

*A beat.*

*A curt, urgent shout;*

Victor!

VICTOR: M'sieur?

DORIAN: Could you ask Mrs. Leaf and two of the staff to join me please.

VICTOR: M'sieur.

*The FOOTMEN (rolling up their shirt-sleeves for work), MRS LEAF and VICTOR report for duty.*

DORIAN: *(Quite calmly.)* Thank you gentlemen…

THE FOOTMEN: *(As if they were shouldering a heavy weight.)* **Ouf!!**

## SCENE THIRTEEN
## ON THE BACK STAIRS, GROSVENOR SQUARE

*The FOOTMEN say their lines as if they were under the physical strain of carrying a very heavy object up a flight of twisting stairs.*

**CHORUS; *"THE OLD SCHOOLROOM."***

VICTOR: Very heavy, it looked. No, I did not ask.

MRS.LEAF: The old schoolroom Mr Dorian?, I said. Oh but that's full of dust –

1ˢᵀ FOOTMAN: Tricky to get up the stairs – and with that bloody great cloth thing all over it.

MRS. LEAF: Not fit for you to see sir, not fit indeed. The key, sir?

2ᴺᴰ FOOTMAN: Said he didn't want the frame scratched.

1ˢᵀ FOOTMAN: Right to the top of the fucking house no less.

MRS. LEAF: Where he hadn't been since he was a *little* boy...

2ᴺᴰ FOOTMAN: Mind if I have a look, sir? Oh – right you are sir, sorry I asked...

MRS. LEAF: I took it to him with the evening paper –

*(Conspiratorially.)* "Inquest on an Actress – "

1ˢᵀ FOOTMAN: "Miss Sybil Vane – ..."

VICTOR: "...Death by 'Misadventure.'"

2ᴺᴰ FOOTMAN: Mother grieves; Brother sails for Australia;

FRANCIS: Thank you.

ALL: No... Witnesses... Summoned –

*The loud click of a heavy lock.*

*THE MEN drop into their own voices. The picture is now in the attic.*

*Safe.*

*Safe.*

ALL: *Nothing's as safe as a locked room... Don't you find?*

*The staff return to their work. MRS LEAF and FRANCIS remain eavesdropping.*

## SCENE FOURTEEN
## THE PICTURE IN THE ATTIC

*DORIAN uncovers the picture, to see what effect the scene with BASIL has had on it.*

*A silence. He lets the pall fall back over the picture. He sits in a chair to think.*

**MRS LEAF'S CHORUS: "NO EYE BUT HIS WOULD EVER SEE HIS SHAME."**

FRANCIS: *Evil. Evil, in those bright blue eyes.*

MRS LEAF: *The coarse stare of cheap little renter.*

FRANCIS, IN A RENTER'S VOICE: **"You show me yours, and I might show you mine"**

MRS LEAF: *Shameful.*

FRANCIS: *But what did that matter?*

MRS LEAF: *What did it matter; no one would ever see it –* **He** *would never see it. Why should he? Why should he watch his soul being called to judgement?*

*And besides, there was no reason that the future should be full of shame. Of sin...*

*She slides into MRS. LEAF's voice;*

**You wouldn't be thinking of living up there would you sir I said, not in a room you haven't entered since you were a little boy, not since your uncle's day, who was so fond of you sir, so fond he was...of the little boy...up there...**

*She leaves an uncomfortable pause to see if DORIAN will respond to this dangerous memory; DORIAN flinches, but does not speak.*

**...and you so comfortable down here. No, he said. No.**

**People talk about secret vices; personally, I think there are no such things.**

*No such things. If a man has a vice, it writes itself across his face –*

DORIAN: *(Shouting down from the attic.)* Thank you Mrs Leaf!

Thank you, everyone. That will be all.

*Everyone leaves, except VICTOR, who pauses on his exit to lurk and watch, taking care that he can't be seen; it is the first time that the stage has been this empty.*

*DORIAN looks at the audience.*

## SCENE FIFTEEN
## THE SECRET LIFE OF DORIAN GRAY

*DORIAN talks to the audience – casually, at first, but becoming the silken-voiced Devil himself as he mysteriously walks through the walls of the attic – no lock can be heard turning – and approaches the footlights.*

She has a point, of course. Hour by hour, and week by week, the hideousness of age is in store for us all. Cheeks become hollow, or flaccid. Yellow crow's-feet creep around the fading eyes and make them horrible; hair loses its brightness, mouths gape or droop, they become foolish and gross. The wrinkled throat; the bloated, blue-veined hands – the twisted body...there is no help for it.

How cruel.

But...this body; these hands...this hair...

The worship of the senses has often, it seems to me, been decried. Men feel perhaps a natural terror for those passions and sensations which seem stronger than themselves. So much is surrendered – and to such little purpose. Such monstrous forms of self torture and self denial; such fear; such...degradation. And yet, surely...

Surely, there are few of us who have not wakened before dawn with a terrible sense of the necessity for the continuance of this same wearisome round of stereotyped habits where we had left it off...wakened with a wild longing, it may be, that our eyelids might open some morning upon a world that has been refashioned anew in the darkness of our pleasure...a world in which things would have fresh colours and shapes, and be changed. A world in which the past would have little or no place – or survive, at any rate, in no conscious form of obligation... or of regret.

It is the creation of worlds such as these that seem to me to be the true object – or amongst the true objects – of Life.

And who has not dreamed of that?

*He becomes aware that VICTOR is still present.*

Yes Victor.

VICTOR: *(With a silver tray.)* Tonight's invitations M'sieur.

*DORIAN begins his evening out by leafing through them; this sequence is clearly a well-oiled ritual. He opens one letter with a long-bladed paper-knife.*

DORIAN: No – No – Ah. Lady Bloxham. How old?

VICTOR: Seventeen, I believe.

DORIAN: Do you. But then one can believe – or disbelieve – so much.

VICTOR: Yes m'sieur.

*DORIAN selects a buttonhole from another tray.*

DORIAN: Society, for instance, cannot believe anything to a man's dishonour if he has still the look of one kept unspotted by the world.

VICTOR: No, m'sieur.

DORIAN: Of course, great wealth does also bring with it a certain element of security.

VICTOR: Yes m'sieur.

*On another tray, a small silver box of cocaine, to which DORIAN matter-of-factly helps himself.*

DORIAN: Society is never very ready to believe anything to the detriment of those who are both rich and fascinating; it feels instinctively that manners are more important than morals.

VICTOR: Yes, m'sieur.

DORIAN: And is insincerity such a terrible thing?

VICTOR: No, m'sieur.

DORIAN: I think not. It is merely a method by which we can multiply our personalities.

Victor?

VICTOR: M'sieur?

*Without any warning, DORIAN grabs VICTOR's face and kisses him violently – lasciviously, brutally. The boy reels – DORIAN has bitten his mouth.*

VICTOR: *(Terrified.)*      Monsieur Gray…

DORIAN: *(Shamelessly confronting the audience with a tiger's snarl.)*

**Hour by hour. Week by week.**

**Year, by year, by year…**

## SCENE SIXTEEN
## DORIAN'S PARTY. TWENTY YEARS LATER

*The hiss and crackle of a stylus going down on a record; Alice Delysia singing Gershwin's "Do It Again". We realise that it is now twenty years later.*

*Fireworks explode. A party in Cafe de Paris; greying hair all round – except for the future DUCHESS OF MONMOUTH, a wealthy American heiress who has come over to do the London Season and marry into the peerage. Champagne – party hats – balloons and streamers drift down. A riot.*

*VICTOR cowers as he sees two PRIVATE DETECTIVES approach – they grab him, and FRANCIS pays them to keep their dirty work quiet. DUCHESS OF MONMOUTH is introduced to DORIAN by LORD HENRY. Photographers ask DORIAN and the DUCHESS for a photo; flashbulb. Suddenly the party stops.*

DORIAN: It was the ninth of November, I remember. The evening of my thirty-eighth birthday.

## SCENE SEVENTEEN
## A FOGGY NIGHT IN GROSVENOR SQUARE.

*A man with greying hair and in a heavy overcoat passes DORIAN, and stops in his tracks; it is BASIL – twenty years older.*

*DORIAN's manner has changed again – he is a man who has spent years partying. BASIL has become, if anything, more himself.*

BASIL: Dorian?… It is you. Don't you recognise me? Basil.

DORIAN: In this fog. I can't even recognise Grosvenor Square.

BASIL: I've been waiting for you.

DORIAN: Really.

BASIL: Since nine o'clock. Finally I took pity on your servant and told him to go to bed. I'm off to Paris on the midnight train you see – I'm going to shut myself up and work, at least that's the idea… – Look might I come in, there's something I want to say to you.

DORIAN: Won't you miss your train?

BASIL: I can easily get to Victoria in twenty minutes – and I've sent my luggage on already.

DORIAN: Alright. I have my latch-key, so we needn't wake anybody.

BASIL: Thanks.

*They go into the house.*

What became of your Frenchman, by the way?

DORIAN: Victor? Oh, I never liked him. Brandy and soda?

BASIL: Nothing thanks.

DORIAN: What's it all about then? Not me, I hope. I'm rather tired of myself tonight.

BASIL: I think you should know the most dreadful things are being said against you in London.

DORIAN: Scandals about myself don't interest me.

BASIL: They must interest you. Of course, I don't believe the rumours. At least, I can't believe them when I see you.

DORIAN: Thank you.

BASIL: But I do hear them, and I don't know what to say. Why is it, Dorian, that a man like the Duke of Berwick leaves the room when you enter it? I met him at dinner last week, your name happened to come up in conversation in connection with some miniatures at the Dudley – and he curled his lip and said you were a man no right-minded girl should be allowed to know, and no married woman sit in the same room with. I asked him what he meant, and he told me. He told me right out before everybody. It was horrible.

**The MEN of the CHORUS:** *(Sotto voce.)* **Horrible.**

BASIL: And why is your friendship so fatal to young men? There was that wretched boy in the guards who committed suicide; –

**The MEN of the CHORUS:** *Wretched.*

BASIL: You were his great friend. There was Sir Henry Ashton, who had to leave the country with a tarnished name –

**The MEN of the CHORUS:**          *Tarnished.*

BASIL: and what about Lord Kent's only son, and his career? I met his father yesterday in St James' Street, and he seemed broken with sorrow and shame.

**CHORUS:**          *Broken.*

DORIAN: *(To the voices.)* Stop!!

Stop, Basil. You are talking about things of which you know nothing. If the Duke of Berwick leaves a room when I enter it it is because I know everything about his life, not because he knows anything about mine. You ask me about Henry Ashton and young Kent. Did I teach the one his vices, or the other his debauchery? I know how people chatter in England, but you forget that we are in the native land of the hypocrite.

BASIL: One has the right to judge a man by the effect he has on his friends.

*A pointed silence. When he speaks again, BASIL's voice is full of pain and even sympathy – he still loves him.*

Then there are the other stories. Stories that you have been seen creeping at dawn out of some of the foulest dens in London. –

DORIAN: Please don't touch me.

BASIL: Are they true? I tell people that I know you, that you are incapable of – Know you! I wonder, do I? Before I could answer that, I should have to see your soul.

*A beat.*

DORIAN: See my soul?

BASIL: Yes, but only God can do that.

DORIAN: Really?

*DORIAN picks up a lamp.*

Come upstairs. Basil.

BASIL: *(Thinking that after all these years DORIAN is suggesting that they finally fuck – )* Can't you see what I am going through?! My god, don't tell me it's all true!!

DORIAN: You've chattered enough about corruption. Now you shall look at it face to face.

BASIL: What do you mean?

DORIAN: I keep a diary of my life from day to day, and it never leaves the room in which it is written. If you come upstairs, I will show it you.

BASIL: All I want is a plain answer to my questions.

DORIAN: You won't have to read long, Basil.

*DORIAN puts the paperknife in his pocket. He leads BASIL upstairs.*

*The loud sound of the attic door unlocking; the CHORUS stirs in anticipation.*

*DORIAN takes off his jacket.*

So, you think it is only God who sees the soul, Basil.

BASIL: What are you doing?

*DORIAN pulls the now-rotted embroidered pall from the picture. The attic turns blood-red.*

### CHORUS; THE MURDER

CHORUS: *(The Picture greets its new victim.)*    **Aaaaaah!**

BASIL: Jesus Christ!! Who has done this?

DORIAN: You did, Basil.

BASIL: Never – it's impossible –

CHORUS: *(An animal sound to the voices; lascivious, sneering.)*

**But you did...**

**With every stroke of gold –**

**Every touch of scarlet –**

**And now look; look at it.**

BASIL: I don't believe this is my picture

DORIAN: Can you see your *romance* in it?

CHORUS:    **Look at the hands...**

**Bestial. Sodden.**

> *Sodden and Shameful.*
>
> *Shameful – Sinful… Sinful!*

DORIAN: Look at it!

CHORUS: *Look at the eyes…*

> *still lovely, but –*
>
> *In the eyes, Joy.*
>
> *The flicker of Triumph.*

BASIL: No. You were my ideal. There was nothing shameful in what I saw in you. Nothing!

CHORUS: *You worshipped him.*

BASIL: What does it mean? Dorian? What does it mean!!

Pray with me.

*BASIL sits in the chair and starts praying.*

Our Father, who art in Heaven…

DORIAN: It is too late for that, Basil.

CHORUS: *(Sotto voce.)* *Hallowed be thy name… Thy kingdom come,*

BASIL: It is never too late.

CHORUS: *Thy will be done, on Earth as it is in Heaven. Give us this day, our daily –*

*DORIAN has already stripped to the waist so as not to ruin his clothes with blood, and now gets ready with the paperknife.*

DORIAN: Each of us has Heaven and Hell in him, Basil!!!

*DORIAN stabs BASIL in the neck and holds him in the chair while he bleeds out. Some of the CHORUS amplify his death-throes, making them sound strangely sexual; others implacably finish the Pater Noster as BASIL slowly and messily dies.*

CHORUS: *…our daily bread, and forgive us our trespasses, as we forgive those who trespass against us…*

*Who trespass.*

*Lead us not into temptation, but…*

*Lead us not, but deliver us...*

*Deliver us...*

*Deliver us from...*

*Finally the jerking stops; BASIL is dead.*

CHORUS: ...... *Amen.*

*DORIAN is covered in blood. He goes to leave.*

FRANCIS: *(Stonily.)* **The lamp.**

*DORIAN stops, thinks, collects the lamp and goes back downstairs and puts it back where it should be. He thinks again.*

FRANCIS: **No one saw him come into the house. And he said he'd sent his luggage on to Paris already. Do it.**

*DORIAN wipes off the blood as best he can, and then puts his coat and scarf back on and goes outside. He knocks on the door, outside, then calls out.*

DORIAN: Francis!

*FRANCIS re-assumes his role as if he neither knew or had seen a thing. He opens the front door.*

Sorry to wake you, but I seem to have forgotten my latch key. What time is it?

FRANCIS: *(In a dressing gown, sleepily.)* Five minutes past two, sir

DORIAN: How horribly late – did anyone call?

FRANCIS: A Mr Hallward, sir. He stayed until eleven, then went away to catch his train.

DORIAN: Oh? I'm sorry I didn't see him. Please call me at nine tomorrow Francis.

FRANCIS: Yes sir.

DORIAN: No later, I have some work I must do.

FRANCIS: Yes sir. Goodnight sir.

*FRANCIS leaves – or rather, re-joins the CHORUS.*

*In the attic, BASIL's dead body is slumped in the chair in front of the picture.*

*A clock chimes two forty-five a.m...*

*Unable to stand the silence, DORIAN puts on a jazz record – a tinny, nasty sound. He starts to clean the paperknife, manically scrubbing away the blood.*

*The CHORUS – all of them – wait, sitting in a debris of balloons and streamers.*

*The Picture waits in the dark.*

MRS LEAF: ***Hours.***

       ***Weeks.***

       ***Years...***


*Curtain.*

*Interval.*

# ACT TWO

SCENE EIGHTEEN
GROSVENOR SQUARE. THE NEXT MORNING

*Cold white light on empty chairs and debris. Streamers, balloons, champagne. The body is still there – staring at the picture – but the chairs the CHORUS were sitting in when the curtain came down are all empty. The stage is dominated by the picture, backlit against the dawn.*

*The needle clicks and clicks as the gramophone record spins round.*

*ALAN is just finishing his costume change from a Photographer (his last appearance) into ALAN CAMPBELL. He then stands and waits to play his role.*

*MRS LEAF is tidying up. She pauses.*

MRS LEAF: **Years… Weeks…**

**Hours.**

*A clock chimes ten. FRANCIS enters with a tray of champagne for two.*

FRANCIS: I awoke him at nine, as instructed – and he gave me a card;

*(He reads it.)* "Alan Campbell – 152 Hertford Street WC1" – …who used to be his *friend*. Some sort of chemist, I think. I sent one of the boys round.

*DORIAN enters drying himself from a shower; a gorgeous silk dressing gown. Sunshine incarnate, apparently.*

Mr Campbell is in the library Sir.

DORIAN: Thank you.

*FRANCIS ushers ALAN in.*

Alan, this is kind of you.

*ALAN will not speak while FRANCIS is in the room. FRANCIS leaves.*

ALAN: Your note said it was a matter of life and death.

DORIAN: Yes, and to more than one person. Do sit down.

Alan, in a locked room at the top of this house – a room to which no one but myself has access – there is a dead man seated in a chair. Don't look at me like that; who the man is, why he died and how he died are matters that do not concern you. What you have to do is this;

ALAN: Stop. I decline entirely to be mixed up in your life, Gray. Your poisonous secrets no longer interest me.

*ALAN goes to leave.*

DORIAN: I'm afraid they'll have to, Alan. Nobody saw this man come into the house; he will not be missed for months – but when he is, there must be no trace of him found here. Now I know you are scientific, know all about anatomy and chemicals and that kind of thing – I've followed your work in the newspapers you see. Ever since our…falling-out.

ALAN: Those days are dead.

DORIAN: The dead linger, Alan. I want you to change this man upstairs into a handful of ashes that I may scatter in the air.

ALAN: I absolutely refuse.

DORIAN: Then I am afraid you leave me no choice.

*He hands ALAN a letter in an envelope.*

You see the address. How is your mother, Alan?

ALAN: Dorian –

DORIAN: Ah! I've been waiting for you to call me Dorian.

ALAN: You're insane.

DORIAN: Quite possibly. Francis!

FRANCIS: *(Entering.)* Sir?

DORIAN: What is the name of that man down at Richmond who supplies our orchids, Francis?

FRANCIS: Harden, sir.

DORIAN: Mr. Harden, yes. Well I want you to go down to Richmond personally and tell Mr. Harden to send twice as many orchids as I ordered. And just before you do that, Mr

Campbell is going to write you a short list of some things he requires brought round from Hertford Street – some chemicals and so on. How long will your experiment take do you think Alan? –

ALAN: About five hours.

DORIAN: In which case, Francis, you may have the evening to yourself. I shall dine out. *(Proffering pen.)* Alan?

*ALAN writes the list, and passes it to FRANCIS.*

*FRANCIS goes to leave.*

And Francis –

FRANCIS: Sir?

DORIAN: As few *white* ones as possible, tell Mr Harden. In fact, no white ones at all.

FRANCIS: Very good.

*FRANCIS leaves.*

DORIAN: Right…

*MRS LEAF and FRANCIS suddenly glare; DORIAN, as if sensing their prompt, stops in his tracks – he has just remembered that he has left the picture uncovered. He could collapse under the pressure of having to go back upstairs.*

ALAN: Shall we go up then?

DORIAN: In a moment, Alan. Do help yourself while I'm gone.

*DORIAN goes upstairs; braces himself; and the moment he unlocks the door, the still uncovered picture whispers and leers at him;*

**CHORUS; THE MURDER (2). MRS LEAF AND FRANCIS**

DORIAN: *(Recoiling in shock.)* Ah!!

CHORUS: ***Yes!!! Blood – fresh blood, all over its hands. As if the canvas was sweating with it.***

DORIAN: God in heaven!

CHORUS: ***God? God?!?***

*(Implacable, accusing.)* ***Our Father, which art in heaven, hallowed be thy name. Forgive us our trespasses, as we***

*forgive those who trespass against us; lead us not into temptation, and deliver us from –*

DORIAN: Ah!!!

*DORIAN throw the pall over the picture, silencing the terrible voices in his head…*

*Downstairs, FRANCIS has returned with ALAN's Gladstone bag and his surgeon's case of tools.*

FRANCIS: *(Calling up.)* Sir?

DORIAN: *(Calling down.)* Thank you Francis. You can come up now Alan.

*FRANCIS leaves. ALAN goes upstairs. He stops with shock in the doorway, but then, apparently unperturbed by the body, he takes off his jacket and starts to roll up his sleeves.*

DORIAN: You have saved me from ruin, Alan. I shan't forget that.

ALAN: You should leave now.

DORIAN: Yes.

*ALAN opens his bag, dons a rubber apron and starts work on stripping the body. Barely keeping himself together, DORIAN walks to the footlights. With all the shaken bravado he can muster, his mask is forced back on;*

DORIAN: **Sometimes… Sometimes, one does feel so keenly the pleasures of a double life.**

*His hands are shaking so badly he can't even get his gold cigarette case open.*

**Don't you find.**

*A burst of laughter and applause, as if that was the curtain line of a play….*

**Thank you.**

*LORD HENRY enters to watch; he too now has grey hair.*

*DORIAN shouts to whoever might hear him to please start the next scene and rushes off –*

**Do excuse me.**

**Thank you!!!**

## SCENE NINETEEN
## A WEST END FOYER – AGAIN.... FIVE YEARS LATER

*Applause. The Ladies sweep on to distract from the horrors of what is happening to BASIL's body. The staging of the scene – like many of its lines – repeats the first foyer scene, showing how these people have remained trapped as they have aged. Everyone is visibly older than they were in Act One. Ladies NARBOROUGH and RUXTON and MRS. ERLYNNE have dessicated; LADY CARLISLE is even stouter, and her stream-of-consciousness chatter now verges on senility; LADY WOTTON has become a stoically mannered drunk and addict, bearing all the scars of having been married to HENRY for decades – her voice is a cracked record stuck in the Wildean days of her youth. The American Heiress has now become the Duchess of Monmouth, having added the Duke's social position to her money.*

*The actors playing JAMES and VICTOR are in evening dress, and repeat the moves of The Two Stage-door Johnnies from the first foyer scene – except that this time they go off arm in arm. It is the 1920s, after all. If the play in the first foyer scene was imagined to be Wilde's* An Ideal Husband, *this time it is Coward's* The Vortex.

*THE DUCHESS OF MONMOUTH is loitering with intent – she is infatuated with DORIAN.*

*Later in the scene, BASIL and ALAN, now both dead, return to haunt DORIAN.*

*LORD HENRY is onstage, but not in the scene. He and DORIAN no longer go to the theatre together.*

LADY NARBOROUGH: Goodness, *what* an ugly story.

LADY RUXTON: Do you like it?

LADY NARBOROUGH: Oh yes. So far. Do you?

LADY RUXTON: Oh yes. *Dreadfully* superficial.

MRS. ERLYNNE:  Dreadfully. What martyrs we are.

LADY CARLISLE: Lady Monmouth! – Oh a thousand pardons, I didn't see you hadn't finished your cigarette.

LADY MONMOUTH: Not at all Lady Carlisle, I smoke a great deal too much. I keep on promising to limit myself in the future.

LADY CARLISLE: How wise.

LADY WOTTON: Pray don't Lady Monmouth; moderation is fatal. Enough is as bad as a meal. More than enough is as good as a feast.

LADY MONMOUTH: You must explain that to me some time, Lady Wotton. It sounds a fascinating theory.

LADY WOTTON: Yes it is.

LADY CARLISLE: How horrid of Mr Gray to miss the first act. He promised not to disappoint.

MRS ERLYNNE: Perhaps, he is in love.

*She drifts away to her next drink or fix. DORIAN enters the foyer, dressed to the nines, his face stony.*

LADY NARBOROUGH: Or abroad.

LADY RUXTON: He is certainly full of surprises still.

MRS ERLYNNE: He flirts disgracefully.

LADY RUXTON: Yes, he is very fascinating.

LADY NARBOROUGH: He is very modern.

LADY CARLISLE: Why isn't he married?

*DORIAN enters, immaculate, smiling.*

DORIAN: You must go through DeBretts, Lady Carlisle, and draw up a list of all the eligible young ladies.

LADY CARLISLE: With their ages, Mr. Gray?

DORIAN: Of course. Slightly edited.

LADY WOOTON: What nonsense, people talk about happy marriages. A man can be happy with any woman, as long as he doesn't love her.

LADY CARLISLE: Oh, Mr Gray, I do wish someone would tell me how to retain my youth…

DORIAN: Well…; can you remember any great errors that you committed in your early days, Lady Carlisle?

LADY CARLISLE: Oh dear; any *errors*…?

**DEAD BASIL: Yes; errors.**

*FRANCIS rings a bell to announce the end of the interval.*

LADY CARLISLE: D'you know, I'm not at all sure I can… The years, Mr. Gray – the years.

Whatever became of that nice Mr Campbell of yours, by the way?

*A second bell.*

**DEAD ALAN: He killed himself.**

DORIAN: Oh, he killed himself.

LADY CARLISLE: Strange choices some people make.

DORIAN: Indeed.

**DEAD BASIL: Indeed. What martyrs we are. And what about the brother?**

*A third bell.*

**DEAD ALAN: Whose brother?**

**DEAD BASIL: Sybil's.**

**MRS LEAF: The little "actress".**

**DEAD ALAN: Oh, him; "still safely in Australia."**

LADY CARLISLE: Might you be disengaged on Tuesday, Mr Gray? It'll just be a small party, got up in rather a hurry – an Ambassador, possibly, and a few young men – all dull I'm afraid, but an old woman like me must have some fresh air. And I've invited the Duchess for you, of course…

*A fourth bell.*

Ah Lady Barford…still with us…Lady Barford!

*LADY CARLISLE bustles off in pursuit of her retreating victim.*

*When the foyer is empty of other women, LADY MONMOUTH makes her move.*

LADY MONMOUTH: Mr. Gray.

DORIAN: Lady Monmouth. And how is the Duke?

LADY MONMOUTH: Still alive. And boring me almost as much as he bores himself.

DORIAN: Ah, nowadays all the married men live like bachelors.

*He offers her a cigarette. The pair of queens crosses the foyer and leaves.*

LADY MONMOUTH: And all the "bachelors" like married men, apparently. Thanks.

DORIAN: Do you ever worry, Lady Monmouth, that you lack the indefineably feminine charm of weakness?

LADY MONMOUTH: Never. *(Flagrantly.)* Shall I see you at Lady Carlisle's?

DORIAN: Perhaps.

*Final Bell!!!!!!*

LADY MONMOUTH: Good!

*LADY MONMOUTH retires. Silence.*

DORIAN: Christ.

*A theatre barman clears away empty glasses. DORIAN down the dregs of a bottle of champagne. LORD HENRY, DEAD BASIL and DEAD ALAN watch DORIAN.*

**DEAD BASIL: You are quite right to do that… "Nothing can cure the soul…but the senses."**

DORIAN: *(To the BARMAN.)* What did you say?

THE BARMAN: Beg your pardon sir?

DORIAN: What did you just say!!

THE BARMAN: Nothing, sir.

*DORIAN mops his brow – he is sweating. He pointlessly gives the barman a big tip from his wallet – reminding us of the other times he has paid people off.*

DORIAN: I see. Well carry on. Thank you!

*Three final bells – under their pressure, DORIAN cracks, and rushes home.*

Francis!!

## SCENE TWENTY
### DORIAN'S HOUSE. LATER THAT NIGHT

*With LORD HENRY watching – he has dropped by for a nightcap – DORIAN ransacks his room looking for some coke, he finds his stashbox and scrapes it out, but it is not enough to satisfy him. Meanwhile, DEAD ALAN and DEAD BASIL speak inside his head. DORIAN is in a very private hell of paranoia, and barely acknowledges their voices, or LORD HENRY's presence. He checks he has enough cash in his wallet to score, and puts on his coat. He is sweaty, jumpy, messy; busy, aggressive, offhand, snappy. An addict who needs his next fix.*

DEAD BASIL: **Soul.**

DEAD ALAN: **Senses.**

DEAD BASIL: **Senses –**

DEAD ALAN: **Soul…**

DEAD BASIL: **They say that passion does make us think in a circle. The things that one longs for, one sometimes loathes.**

DEAD ALAN: **The things that fascinate, make us afraid…**

DEAD BASIL: **And the brain of course has its own food, on which it must batten. Its own hungers!**

DEAD ALAN: **The imagination can twist like a thing in pain; dance like some foul puppet on a stand.**

DEAD BASIL: **Time…**

DEAD BASIL, DEAD ALAN & MRS LEAF: **Can stop.**

DORIAN: Francis!!

*No response.*

Francis!!!

LORD HENRY: *(Forced to help himself to a cigarette; to DORIAN.)* You ran off very early last night. Did you go on anywhere fascinating?

DORIAN: I went to my club, and returned home at exactly ten minutes past two. How odd that you always want to know what one has been doing, while I always want to forget.

LORD HENRY: My dear boy; as if I care…

FRANCIS: *(Outside the scene.)* **Yes Sir?**

DORIAN: A cab. – I'll give him the address.

FRANCIS: **Of course.**

LORD HENRY: You don't seem quite yourself, that's all.

DORIAN: Each man lives his own life, and each man pays his own price for living it. The only pity is that one has to pay so often.

LORD HENRY: Tomorrow at tea time then? The Duchess is coming.

DORIAN: Don't worry about me Harry!!

In three days, I'll be fine.

FRANCIS: **Your cab, sir.**

DORIAN: Yes. Thank you. *(Starting the next scene as he exits.)* Thank you!!

*DORIAN leaves. The slamming of a cab door. The cab drives off.*

**LORD HENRY:** *(To the audience.)* Really, by this point, I was his only friend…

## SCENE TWENTY-ONE

*CHORUS; THE JOURNEY TO LIMEHOUSE*

*The DUCHESS dresses for dinner. The dead linger.*

DEAD BASIL: **There is a fear which can seem, at times, almost too great to be born…**

**Sometimes, he could forget the picture, get back his light heart, find himself able for a time to rejoice in the fact that the wonderful beauty that had so fascinated Basil Hallward –**

DEAD ALAN: **And so many others –**

DEAD BASIL: – seemed never to leave him. But then, returning home, he would go back up to that locked, lonely room, and sit in front of it, loathing both it and himself, gazing at the misshapen shadow which now had to bear the burden which should have been his own. How long ago that summer day now seemed on which it had been painted…a day filled with the odour of roses, the heavy scent of lilac, and the more delicate scent of the flowering thorn… He felt a pity all the more poignant because it was so purely selfish.

MRS LEAF: I used to hear crying, upstairs.

DUCHESS: Yes, I used to hear the stories. Stories that he'd been seen in dreadful places down by the docks where they said you could buy oblivion.

MRS LEAF: Sometimes we didn't see him for three whole days.

DUCHESS: I never went myself. Did he? I didn't ask.

MRS LEAF: And what about those bars he had put across the old school-room door, and the locks, when he was away? What were *they* for, eh?

DUCHESS: Secrecy is the one thing that can make modern life marvellous, after all. Or whatever it was we all used to say. In those days.

*A taxi-door slams.*

*The red lights of Limehouse appear.*

*DORIAN enters, in disguise.*

FRANCIS: *(As cab-driver.)* We're 'ere, Sir…

MRS LEAF: I saw him. I saw him, in his hat and coat. Creeping…

## SCENE TWENTY-TWO
## LIMEHOUSE

*DORIAN talks to the audience about Limehouse, justifying his life there. As he talks, the characters for this scene assemble; working girls and their clients.*

DORIAN: **The desire to live... The wild desire to live is the most terrible of all appetites, quickening into force every trembling nerve...**

**That, and the hunger for rebellion.**

**Ugliness, once hateful because it made things real, becomes dear, and for that very reason. Ugliness is the one Reality. The coarse brawl, the crude violence of a disordered life, the vileness of Thief and Outcast...are more vivid, to me – more vivid, in their intense actuality, than all the...all the...**

**They become what one *needs*.**

*The MADAM hovers with her staff. DORIAN knows that they are there.*

DORIAN: Get the stuff ready. And some water.

MADAM: Of course.

PROSTITUTE 1: ...'ere, 'andsome...do you love me? I love you.

DORIAN: No. I am sick of women who love me. Women who hate one are so much more interesting.

PROSTITUTE 2: We're very proud tonight.

DORIAN: For God's sake don't talk to me! *(Gives them money.)* Don't ever talk to me again.

MADAM: *(Prompting the girls.)* Thank you.

PROSTITUTE 2: Thank you Mr Gray...

DORIAN: Don't call me that.

PROSTITUTE 2: Alright...!

PROSTITUTE 1: Prince Charming, that's what you like to be called, ain't it...

*A face-down sailor lifts his head;*

MADAM: Out. Now! *(To DORIAN.)* There we are.

*She hands DORIAN his drugs. He gazes at them lovingly.*

**THE DUCHESS, IN DEAD SYBILS' VOICE: Now I've got you, I don't need anything else.**

*The sailor staggers to his feet; it is JAMES VANE.*

DORIAN: *(Looking at the drugs, laughing.)* How perfectly true.

**THE DUCHESS, IN DEAD SYBIL'S VOICE: Prince… Charming…**

*DORIAN laughs, and prepares to jack up.*

*JAMES grabs him from behind, and holds a gun to his head.*

JAMES: Quiet, or I shoot.

DORIAN: What do you want. What have I ever done to you –

JAMES: Sybil Vane was my sister, *Prince Charming* – *(He cocks the pistol.)*

**FIRST PROSTITUTE: Do it!!**

JAMES: Now make your peace with God, because I am going to kill you.

DORIAN: I never knew your sister. Never heard of Sybil V – ah!!!

JAMES: One minute.

**MADAM, PROSTITUTES:** *(Quietly, gloating.)* **Our Father, which art in Heaven, etc.**

*The Pater Noster builds in intensity towards the expiry of the minute – one of the prostitutes laughs – then –*

DORIAN: Wait! Wait – How long is it – *(He chokes.)*

*The CHORUS' praying breaks off.*

JAMES: How long is it what?

DORIAN: How long is it since your sister died.

JAMES: Why?

DORIAN: How many years since she died? Tell me!

JAMES: Twenty-five. Twenty-five long, empty years. But what do years matter –

DORIAN: Look at my face.

**THE WOMEN: *Do it now!***

DORIAN: For god's sake look at my face!!!!

*JAMES does – and recoils in horror. The CHORUS are dismayed – a beast cheated of its prey.*

DORIAN: Twenty-five years you said.

JAMES: Jesus Christ. Jesus Christ I would have killed you.

DORIAN: You'd better go home, or you might get into trouble.

JAMES: I will sir.

DORIAN: And let this be a warning to you not to take vengeance into your own hands.

JAMES: Yes sir thank you sir.

*DORIAN steps out onto the street, gulping the night air.*

**CHORUS: *Safe.***

MADAM: You fool; you should have killed him when you had the chance.

JAMES: The man whose life I want must be over forty by now – this one's little more than a boy.

PROSTITUTE 1: A boy, him! It's nigh on twenty years since Prince Charming made me what I am.

JAMES: *(Suddenly suspicious.)* You're lying.

PROSTITUTE 1: Twenty years… Christ!! He hasn't changed – I have though… *(She laughs.)* They say 'e made the devil's bargain.

PROSTITUTE 2: He's the worst one comes in 'ere.

PROSTITUTE 1: You won't tell him she said that, will you. We're afraid of him. Couldn't let me have some money for my night's lodgings could you mister?

JAMES: *(Breaking away.)* Damn Him!! Damn him…

*Enter LORD HENRY.*

**JAMES:** *(As CHORUS.)* **Damn him...to hell...**

**LORD HENRY:** *(Carrying and quoting from a copy of* The Importance of Being Earnest.*)*

**"The good end happily, and the bad, unhappily. That is what Fiction means".**

**In actual *life* of course, as we know, the wicked are not punished, nor the good rewarded. Actual life is chaos. But there is something terribly logical in the Imagination... It is imagination, I fancy, and imagination alone, that sets Remorse to dog the feet of Sin; which causes Crime to bear it misshapen brood of creatures – Fear; Distrust; Terror.**

**Terror.**

DORIAN: Twenty five years!!!...twenty-five...and all of them, all of them have to be paid for.

Nobody knew my real name at the theatre. He cannot possibly know where to find me.

**MADAM:** *(As CHORUS.)* **Of course not.**

**PROSTITUTE:** *(As CHORUS.)* **Of course not, *Mr Gray*...**

*DORIAN hears those voices. Now he is terrified.*

DORIAN: Francis. Francis!!

FRANCIS: Sir?

DORIAN: The yacht. Have the yacht got ready. Or would the country place be safer do you think. The country. Yes. The country. I could invite some people down...

FRANCIS: Sir?

DORIAN: Pack for a whole weekend. Now. I said Now!!

FRANCIS: Sir.

*Gunshots.*

## SCENE TWENTY-THREE
## THE CONSERVATORY AT SELBY ROYAL. A FEW DAYS LATER

*The brutal sounds of a pheasant shoot fade away.*

*The DUCHESS OF MONMOUTH is in white, and angry with herself for still pursuing her affair with this impossible man (and also, I feel sure, for agreeing to spend another country weekend amongst English Society at his house).*

*The staff who brought the tea retire. LADY MONMOUTH reluctantly officiates. Through gritted teeth;*

LADY MONMOUTH: Cake, or bread and butter?

DORIAN: *(In his blackest mood.)* Bread and butter. Please.

*They do not talk.*

*Enter LORD HENRY. He senses the flinty atmosphere, but decides – as ever – to make light of it, while – as ever – observing and probing DORIAN and his baffling mood. HENRY is visibly older, and his cigarettes occasionally make him cough.*

LORD HENRY: And what are you two chattering about?

LADY MONMOUTH: The unfortunate accident this morning. Tea?

LORD HENRY: Please. Accident?

LADY MONMOUTH: One of the beaters walked in front of the guns. Dead, apparently.

LORD HENRY: What a dreadful topic for tea-time. What else?

LADY MONMOUTH: Oh, Love.

LORD HENRY: An illusion. And?

*Beat.*

LADY MONMOUTH: *(Refusing to be drawn.)* Art.

LORD HENRY: A malady.

LADY MONMOUTH: Religion.

LORD HENRY: The fashionable substitute for belief.

*Beat.*

LADY MONMOUTH: And…our host.

LORD HENRY: Ah! A charming topic. Indeed, years ago, he was christened *Prince* Charming.

DORIAN: Don't, Harry.

LADY MONMOUTH: Well not this afternoon he isn't. He has just been explaining to me that my husband married me on purely scientific principles, as the best specimen he could find of a modern butterfly.

LORD HENRY: I hope he doesn't stick pins into you.

LADY MONMOUTH: Oh my maid does that, when she is annoyed with me. Dorian – *(She offers tea.)*

DORIAN: What – No.

LORD HENRY: And what does she get annoyed with you about, Lady Monmouth?

LADY MONMOUTH: Oh, the most trivial things. Usually because I come in at ten minutes to nine and tell her that I must be dressed by half past eight.

LORD HENRY: How unreasonable; you should give her warning.

LADY MONMOUTH: I daren't; she invents hats for me. Mostly out of nothing. All good hats are made out of nothing, apparently.

LORD HENRY: Like all good reputations.

LADY MONMOUTH: I wouldn't know. Apparently in this country they are only bestowed on women who have only ever loved once.

LORD HENRY: My dear Gladys one does only ever love once. Difference of object does not alter singleness of passion. We can have in life but one great experience, at best, and the secret of life is to reproduce that experience as often as humanly possible.

*DORIAN begins to laugh…*

LADY MONMOUTH: Even when one has been wounded by it?

LORD HENRY: Especially when one has been wounded by it.

LADY MONMOUTH: Why are you laughing?

DORIAN: Oh…because I agree with Harry.

LADY MONMOUTH: Even when he is wrong.

DORIAN: Harry is never wrong.

LADY MONMOUTH: And does his philosophy make you happy?

DORIAN: *(An acid outburst.)* I have never searched for happiness. Who wants happiness? I have searched for pleasure.

*A silence.*

LADY MONMOUTH: And found it?

DORIAN: Far too often.

LADY MONMOUTH: Well I am searching for peace. And if I don't go and dress, I shall have none this evening.

*She waits a beat for DORIAN to say "Don't go". He doesn't.*

Might you bring me up some orchids, Lord Henry. Mr Gray's gardener tells me he has some marvellous spotted thing in the conservatory here as effective as the seven deadly sins. I forget the name. I'm sure it was something dreadful. But then, we have quite lost the faculty for giving lovely names to things, haven't we. Nowadays.

*The DUCHESS leaves.*

LORD HENRY: How fond women are of doing dangerous things. It is one of the qualities in them I admire most. Do you love her?

DORIAN: No. Sometimes I *like* her. *(With cold licentiousness.)* Sometimes, very much indeed...

LORD HENRY: Well she loves you – very much – and likes you hardly at all. I should say you were excellently matched.

DORIAN: This business with the beater – it's a bad omen Harry. A bad omen. I feel as if something horrible were going to happen.

LORD HENRY: The only horrible thing in the world is *ennui,* Dorian. *That* is the one sin for which there is no forgiveness. Besides, what on earth could happen to you, and here in the country of all places. You have everything that a man can want – this house... There is no one who would not be delighted to change places with you.

DORIAN: No.

*A beat.*

LORD HENRY: What?

DORIAN: I wish I could love. Or escape. Or…forget.

LORD HENRY: My dear boy do tell me what it is.

**FRANCIS and MRS LEAF:** *Death. The coming of Death.*

DORIAN: My nerves are dreadfully out of order. That's all. I see a lot of blood.

*(Rings bell.)* You will make my excuses at dinner, won't you. I'd better not come down.

LORD HENRY: There is no such thing as an omen, Dorian. Destiny sends no heralds.

*As he goes, he starts coughing, rather badly.*

She's too wise for that. Or too cruel. Sleep well!

*As he exits, we see that LORD HENRY is in fact rather ill.*

FRANCIS: Shall I clear, sir?

DORIAN: Please. Do we know who the man was?

FRANCIS: The man sir?

DORIAN: Who died. I should send some money to his family.

FRANCIS: The Estate men said they'd never seen him sir. I did hear mention that he seemed to be a sailor or colonial of some kind; sunburnt, tattooed on both arms, that kind of thing.

DORIAN: *(Concealing his feelings.)* What? Anything found on him?

FRANCIS: Sir?

DORIAN: *(Sharply.)* Was anything found on him that would tell us his *name*?

FRANCIS: No sir, just his clothes. A decent looking man, but rough – like. It seems he –

DORIAN: Well where is the body? Quick! Quick!!!

*A covered body is wheeled onto the stage on a hospital gurney.*

**MRS LEAF:** *They do say a body brings bad luck –*

**FRANCIS:** *But a terrible hope fluttered past him –*

**MRS LEAF:** *and he clutched at it. "Quick" he said, "Quick – I must see it at once." In the doorway, he paused, knowing that this would be the moment that would either make or mar his life.*

## SCENE TWENTY-FOUR
### A MORGUE *AND* A HOTEL LOBBY IN LONDON OR PARIS…

DORIAN: I felt as if my heart had suddenly stopped beating…

"Take that thing off his face," I said. "I wish to – "

No;

"I *need*…to see it."

*The face of the corpse is uncovered.*

**CHORUS: James…Vane.**

DORIAN: Ah! …Ah!!!

*He weeps with sheer relief….*

**MRS LEAF: *Safe.***

**FRANCIS: *Safe.***

**AND DORIAN: *Safe!!!* /** Safe!!!

LADY MONMOUTH: *(Brazening out that fact that the affair is now over.)* The last time I saw him, there were tears in his eyes. I rather think they were tears of joy.

*A HOTEL MANAGER brings LADY MONMOUTH a box; she snaps at him;*

What?

THE HOTEL MANAGER: From a Mr Gray, ma'am?

*The DUCHESS reads the card with a bitter smile, then opens the box. She starts to laugh – DORIAN has finally sent her her orchids…*

*Through her laughter, music; Noel Coward's "Mad About the Boy". Another decade has passed, and…*

*A MALE NURSE in a white coat wheels in LORD HENRY – now sick, shrivelled, white-haired and past seventy – in a wheelchair.*

## SCENE TWENTY-FIVE
## A SANATORIUM

*DORIAN wipes the tears from his face, and takes over the wheelchair; the MALE NURSE (who is played by the same actor as VICTOR) sits and waits.*

*LORD HENRY is now a white-haired, cantankerous, grape-guzzling invalid. When excited or upset, he coughs – he is dying of emphysema. There is a cylinder of oxygen should he need it.*

*The stage is bare except for the record player and the chairs, a visiting room in a sanatorium.*

LORD HENRY: There is no use your telling me that you are going to be good. You are quite perfect as you are.

DORIAN: I have done many dreadful things in my life Harry, and I am not going to do any more. In fact, I began my good actions this morning.

LORD HENRY: Where were you this morning?

DORIAN: Just north of Oxford Street.

LORD HENRY: My dear boy, anybody can be good in the country.

DORIAN: Harry –

LORD HENRY: And what was this good action? Or did you say you had done more than one.

DORIAN: I spared somebody.

LORD HENRY: Boy or girl?

DORIAN: Girl – and really quite beautiful. Not of our class, but still. I'd arranged everything – made her fall in love with me, rented somewhere in St John's Wood – and then suddenly decided to leave her just as I'd found her.

LORD HENRY: I should think the novelty of the emotion must have given you a real thrill of pleasure… "Not of our class" – really, Dorian, sometimes you do have the most curiously boyish moods – and I can't say I think much of your attempt at reformation from a *moral* point of view. Will this young creature ever be contented now with anyone from her class? She will not. Even at this moment, she is probably drinking the last of the money you doubtless gave her in some vile public house. Later I imagine she will go on to a whole new career working just off the Strand and eventually throw herself into the Thames in pure pique and despair. If people still do that sort of thing.

DORIAN: *(Laughing.)* Please don't try and persuade me that the first good action I have done in years is really a sort of sin. Tell me something about yourself.

LORD HENRY: People here say the newspapers are discussing poor Basil's disappearance again – after all these years. The English police insist he left for Paris by the midnight train, the French police declare he never arrived in Paris at all. I expect eventually we shall be told he has been seen in San Francisco. Everyone who disappears is said to be seen in San Francisco, nowadays. It must be a delightful city *(He coughs.)* and possess all the attractions of the next world.

DORIAN: What do you think happened to Basil?

LORD HENRY: I haven't the slightest idea and I don't want to think about him. Death terrifies me. I hate it.

DORIAN: Why?

LORD HENRY: Because one can survive everything nowadays except Death. That, and vulgarity... Let's have our coffee in the music room...you can play some Chopin for me. A man my wife once ran away with played Chopin, exquisitely. Poor Victoria – of course married life is merely a habit, but then one regrets the loss of even one's worst.

*DORIAN puts on a record; again the same piece of Chopin music that we heard the day these two men met.*

DORIAN: What would you say if I told you that I had murdered Basil?

LORD HENRY: I should say that you were posing for a character that doesn't suit you. Murder is always a mistake. One should never do anything that one cannot talk about after dinner... *(His memory is stirred by the music – he*

*remembers the day the picture was painted.)* Ah!… Strange
how a man could paint like Velásquez and yet be as dull
as possible… I dare say he fell off an omnibus into the
Seine and the conductor hushed it up. By the way, what
became of that wonderful portrait he did of you? Stolen or
something, I remember you said… Did you ever advertise
for it? You should.

DORIAN: I forget. I never really liked it. "Like the painting of
a sorrow, A face without a heart".

LORD HENRY: *Hamlet* Act Four.

By the way, what does it profit a man if he gain the whole
world and lose his own soul?

*A beat.*

DORIAN: Why do you ask me that, Harry?

LORD HENRY: Because I thought you might be able to give
me an answer. I was being wheeled through the Park
last Sunday and heard some shabby little street preacher
yelling that question to his audience. It struck me as rather
dramatic.

DORIAN: The soul is a terrible reality Harry. It can be bought,
and sold, and…bartered away. It can be poisoned.

LORD HENRY: Don't be so serious. What have you or I to
do with the superstitions of the age… Look at you – only
ten years younger than me and here am I, wrinkled and
worn and yellow, while you… You really are wonderful,
Dorian. You have never looked more charming. You
remind me of the day I saw you first. You were rather
cheeky, very shy, and absolutely extraordinary. You have
changed, of course, but not in appearance. I wish you
would tell me your secret. To get back my youth I would
do anything in the world – except take exercise, get up
early or be respectable. *(LORD HENRY has a terrible coughing
fit.)* Youth! there is nothing like it. It's absurd to talk of the
ignorance of youth. The only people to whose opinions
I listen now with any respect are people much younger
than myself. They seem in front of me. As for the aged, I

always contradict the aged. If you ask them their opinion of something that happened yesterday, they solemnly give the opinions of fifty years ago, when people believed in everything and knew absolutely nothing. The tragedy of old age is not that one is old, but that one is young!

*LORD HENRY is almost in tears; tears of rage.*

DORIAN: Harry?

LORD HENRY: I am amazed sometimes at my own sincerity.

What an exquisite life you have had. Nothing has been hidden from you…and it has all been to you no more than the sound of music. You are still the same.

DORIAN: I am not the same, Harry.

LORD HENRY: Yes you are. I wonder what the rest of your life will be like. Don't spoil it with renunciations; don't make yourself incomplete –

DORIAN: Sssh, Harry –

LORD HENRY: Listen to me! Life is not governed by will or intention; life is a question of nerves. You may fancy yourself safe, or think yourself strong, but a chance tone of colour in a room or morning sky, a particular perfume that you once loved – a piece of music – I tell you, Dorian, it is on things like these that our lives depend. There are moments when the odour of white lilacs passes suddenly across me, and I have to live the strangest month of my life all over again.

I wish I could change places with you. The world has cried out against us both, but it has always worshipped you. You are what the age is searching for, and what it is afraid it has found.

DORIAN: I hope not. Harry, I'm tired –

*DORIAN goes to leave – LORD HENRY clutches at his hand. Slightly mad.*

LORD HENRY: Play it for me again. Or perhaps we could go to the club. There is someone at White's who wants to know you immensely – Lord Poole, Bournemouth's youngest –

he's already copied your neck-ties, and has begged me to introduce you. He's quite delightful, and rather reminds me of you.

DORIAN: I want to go to bed early.

LORD HENRY: You know you've never looked so well as you do tonight.

DORIAN: That is because I am going to be good, Harry.

LORD HENRY: My dear boy don't begin to moralise. You and I are what we are. You can never change to me.

*DORIAN indicates to the nurse to wheel LORD HENRY away.*

Perhaps you might take me to the park tomorrow. I don't think there have been such lilacs since the year I met you.

*DORIAN is now alone onstage. LORD HENRY rises from his wheelchair and joins the assembled CHORUS of the Dead.*

DORIAN: Goodbye Harry.

Francis…

FRANCIS: Sir?

*DORIAN gestures for FRANCIS to hand him his old hand mirror.*

DORIAN: Thank you. Oh and Francis –

FRANCIS: Sir?

DORIAN: Tell everyone…that that will be all for tonight. Thank you.

*The CHORUS sit down; they are going nowhere.*

## SCENE TWENTY-SIX
## DORIAN'S HOUSE

*DORIAN holds the same mirror that he first picked up all those years ago, and looks at his face.*

***CHORUS; "A NEW LIFE"***

**DEAD LORD HENRY:** *Is it really true that one can never change?*

*That there is…no hope?*

*Surely it is better not to think of the past. Nothing can alter it. Better to think of oneself, and of one's own future –*

*And consider; James Vane –*

**DEAD JAMES:** *dead in a nameless grave;*

**DEAD LORD HENRY:** *Alan Campbell;*

**DEAD ALAN:** *dead also.*

**DEAD LORD HENRY:** *Basil –*

**DEAD BASIL:** *Forgotten…*

*A beat;*

**DEAD LORD HENRY:** *(The whisper of the tempter…)* *A new life. A New… Life.*

*That is what one wants…*

*DORIAN puts down the mirror.*

**CHORUS:** *That is what one wants, surely.*

*That is what he's waiting for;*

*To be good…*

*(An echo;)* *Good…*

*To not be in terror.*

*(An echo;)* *Terror…*

*To not be in terror of that* thing…

*That thing, upstairs.*

*DORIAN looks in the mirror again. The picture begins to materialise in his mind.*

*And surely, he's begun it already. Surely, the signs of evil will have already begun to fade. Surely it will have changed.*

*Surely.*

*Changed…*

*He puts the mirror down and considers going to check if the picture has changed.*

*Yes; that's it…*

> *Changed – and already. Already, better.*
>
> > *Already –*
>
> *go and look –*
>
> > > *Yes,*
>
> > *that's it; look…*
>
> > *Go and look at it –*


> > > *Look at it.*

*DORIAN moves towards the door of the attic. With the key in the lock, he hesitates, as the chorus urge him on.*

*The unlocking of the door. A pause.*

**DEAD JAMES, THE LIMEHOUSE MADAM:**      *Do it !!!*

*DORIAN braces himself, and uncovers the picture.*

*It has become more terrible.*

DORIAN: *(In pain and indignation.)* Ah!!!

*CHORUS; "THAT KNIFE LOOKS SHARP"*

*CHORUS: (Deliberate; murderous.)*

> *Loathsome –*

*Even more loathsome.*

*Blood on the hands –*

> *More blood –*
>
> > *New blood –*
>
> > > *Fresh blood –*

*Cunning.*

*"I decided to leave her"*

*"I am going to be good."*

*"I am going to change!"*

DORIAN: *No!!!!*

FEMALE CHORUS: *Our Father,*

DEAD BASIL: *Vanity.*

FEMALE CHORUS: *– which art in Heaven,*

DEAD BASIL: *Curiosity.*

FEMALE CHORUS: *– hallowed be thy name.*

DEAD BASIL: *Hypocrisy!!!!…*

FEMALE CHORUS: *Thy Kingdom come, thy will be done, on Earth as it is in Heaven. Give us this day our daily bread, and forgive us our trespasses, as we forgive those*

*Who confess.*

*Confess.*

*CONFESS!!!!!*

*Everything stops. Silence.*

*DORIAN laughs.*

DORIAN: And who would believe me? They'd say I was mad.

MRS LEAF: *There is a God.*

DORIAN: Ha!

CHORUS: *There is a God who calls on men to tell their sins on earth as well as to heaven. It was his duty to confess, to suffer public shame –*

DORIAN: *(Shouting over them; the caged tiger turns on his tormentors.)*

Shame? *Shame!!!!???!!!* And for what?

CHORUS: *Nothing he can do will cleanse him till he has told his own sin. His sin.*

DORIAN: Sin…

*Beat.*

CHORUS: *The murder.*

DORIAN: Is that to dog me all my life? Always, the *past…*

CHORUS: *Confess.*

DORIAN: There's no evidence. No trace. Buried – burnt – forgotten. Everything.

*Beat.*

CHORUS: *The picture.*

DORIAN: What?

CHORUS: *The picture.*

*DORIAN begins to consider…persuasive voices in his ear…;*

> *The picture. Why has he kept it so long? So…long!!*
>
> > *Watching him –*
> >
> > > *Keeping him awake at night –*
> > >
> > > > *Filling him with terror –*
> > > >
> > > > > *Giving him no pleasure –*
> > > > >
> > > > > *The living death of his soul.*

*Beat. DORIAN is handed the knife with which he killed BASIL.*

MRS LEAF: *That knife looks sharp. Not a stain on it.*

*DORIAN looks at the knife.*

CHORUS: *A new life!!*

> *A New… Life!!*

CHORUS: *(To the audience.) And who hasn't dreamed of that…*

*DORIAN raises the knife in a paroxysm of fury and despair, hesitates, and then plunges the blade into the picture.*

*A terrible scream; the knife tears the canvas like skin.*

*Lights blaze, turning the portrait into a looming dark silhouette – the music of the story runs backwards – 1930s jazz turning into the Coward turning into Patti into the Chopin in a bizarre cacophony – as if the years were running backwards –*

CHORUS: *(The terrified babble of the neighbours.)*

**What was that?**

**What was it –**

**Jesus Christ! –**

**Whose house is that?**

**Dorian Gray's**

**Whose?**

**Dorian Gray's**

*DORIAN staggers downstage, away from the canvas. He drops the knife.*

*He turns, and we see that this is in fact some hideous, decayed, liver-spotted old man in shabby, rotted evening dress, blood gurgling from a terrible slash to his face and chest. A nightmare. The voices of the CHORUS thin away into whispers…*

CHORUS: ***Dorian…Gray.***

*and then there is silence.*

*The CHORUS all stare as the blood gurgles in this dying creature's throat.*

*Some of the CHORUS spit on the floor in contempt.*

*MRS. LEAF crosses herself.*

*In the glare of the footlights, the monster dies.*

## SCENE TWENTY-SEVEN
## CODA; THE STAFF GIVE THEIR EVIDENCE

**FOOTMAN 1:** After about a quarter of an hour, I knocked, but there was no reply.

**FOOTMAN 2:** We called out...; nothing.

**FOOTMAN 1:** Finally, after vainly trying to force the door, we got out on the roof, and dropped down onto the balcony. The windows went easily; those bolts were old.

**FOOTMAN 2:** When I went in, up on the wall there was a splendid picture of the master – just as I'd last seen him, in all the wonder of his youth and beauty. And lying on the floor... Jesus Christ it was loathsome.

**FRANCIS:** *(As if each word was a nail in a coffin.)*

***Withered, wrinkled and loathsome.***

**FOOTMAN 1:** *(Putting a handkerchief over his mouth to try and block out the smell of the body.)*

**Mr Francis sir, who in god's name is that? Mr Francis?**

FRANCIS: ***It was not until they examined the rings that they recognised who it was.***

***Cigarette?***

*He offers the audience a cigarette – from DORIAN GRAY's gold cigarette case.*

*As the lights fade, the picture awaits its next victim.*

*Chopin.*

*Blackout.*